Advance Praise for *The UNdepressed Heart*

Cozy up in your favorite chair and have a read with Heather Bailey. She's funny, sensitive, and most of all very real as she talks through the stages of depression and how to nurture yourself through each one. Definitely worth reading and sharing.

—Nancy Bailey

In reading *The UNdepressed Heart*, I learned that I need "me time" and to take care of myself each and every day. I also learned to be more self-aware and the importance of having confidence to get through it.

—Theresa Belt

Reading *The UNdepressed Heart* is like having a personal mentor, life coach, and friend by your side, guiding you through the hard parts so you can step out of the darkness of anxiety and depression into the light of a fully lived life.

In *The UNdepressed Heart*, Heather Bailey shares her journey as a mother, going from the depths of depression to living her life above "heart level." She explains the simple, profound truths that can gently guide any woman out of the pit of depression and back into the light.

As a mother of five myself, I found the author's stories relatable and relevant. The book laid out the stages of depression and healing in an understandable, easy-to-follow format. I didn't think I was depressed (or below heart level) at the beginning of the book, but reading helped me realize that I was, in fact, at a stage below heart level, below a place where I could potentially be living a more joyful, contented life. By following the manageable action steps laid out in each chapter, I brought myself higher than I thought I could go within a stressful life situation, and ultimately to a healthier mental and physical place.

The recommendations in *The UNdepressed Heart* work. The powerful testimony and support found within its pages will give women (mothers or not) and their partners the tools they need to increase their capacity for joy and fulfillment.

—Bree Moore, Author of *Birth Becomes Hers*

The UNdepressed Heart is the answer for ANYONE experiencing depression. Its practical, step-by-step advice can be used to recognize and overcome depression at any stage. As a licensed healthcare professional, I strongly recommend *The UNdepressed Heart* to all who desire to create greater levels of happiness and joy in their lives.

—Eric Bailey

I loved reading Heather Bailey's book, *The UNdepressed Heart!* In it she teaches about the six stages of depression, and what helps most to heal at each level, from various vantage points. These overlap throughout the book, reinforcing the concepts repeatedly with new information.

A young mother herself, Heather writes about experiences other mothers and parents relate to. Her book teaches invaluable tools to help anyone who struggles with depression, grief, or anxiety.

Friends and family of a depressed loved one will benefit from knowing how to best support them in each stage of grief or depression.

Each of us experiences these various stages at times, to one degree or another. Knowing how we can give self-care appropriate for each phase can be literally life-saving!

This is a book every home should have on hand as an emotional first-aid kit.

—Katherine Adamson

A very timely book. I know it will bless MANY families and homes with practical tools and information on *when* and *how* to use them effectively.

—Lisa Davis, Succeed Together Accountability Coach

The book speaks to my heart. I have been so lost and alone. Here in this door I found comfort and peace. It was like I had a little helper I needed to remind me that it's okay and I can. Heather knows how to speak to a woman and knows how to unlock your heart to connect to your mind.

Especially this time of year, I struggle with depression so very bad. And I think I may now have the strength to not merely survive Christmas this year, but I am going to thrive. Being able to open my heart and mind out of the clouds and darkness of depression will be the first time my children will ever experience the true love and joy of this season. Thank you, Heather, for presenting this book, especially at this time of year!!

—Lora Kasteler

The UNdepressed Heart is an astounding book full of inspiration, insight, and real-life experiences. It is written in a way that helps to eliminate the stigma that is sometimes associated with depression and helps to shed light on real solutions. This book has step-by-step instructions to help combat depression in all its stages. It helps readers to see that there is hope and there are possibilities for overcoming the effects of depression. I would strongly recommend *The UNdepressed Heart* to anyone battling depression, anxiety, or negative feelings. This is just the book you need to get back on track and start living your best life!

—Stacie Bundy

Heather Bailey has written an amazing book about coming out of depression. Her vulnerability makes this book life-changing. Her knowledge of the steps up out of depression are transformational and her firsthand experiences show us how passionate and real she is. It just makes a lot of sense that there is a foundational, bottom-up approach to depression that works. I love the clarity she brings to the difference between emotions and feelings and how to apply these differences to our personal relationships for better results. The principles taught in this book are real and they really work. Thank you, Heather!

—Chris Shipley

The UNdepressed Heart is an amazing step-by-step guide through the different stages of depression. It is refreshing to get knowledge about how depression can affect you and how to overcome it. I highly recommend this book to anyone as we go through life and face our demons.

—Andrea Carbine

Life has a way of testing you, and sometimes you feel like you have failed the test before it even starts. I love how Heather Bailey in her book *The UNdepressed Heart* uses examples from her own life, identifies the different levels of depression that a person can go through, and then walks you through ways you can help yourself at each stage and/or prevent yourself from slipping further down those levels.

While I am no longer a new mother, I have experienced enough of what she describes that I readily identified with her descriptions and could see how her suggestions would have been helpful to mitigate the depressive fallout at different crossroads in my life.

Going forward, I am excited to utilize the techniques in this book to better navigate the trials life will inevitably throw at me as well as to better serve those placed in my path. Thank you for the increased awareness and proactive information you have shared via your book, Heather!

—Katherine Bess

I loved reading this book. Losing someone close to you can lead to more feelings than I ever thought I could feel. Depression is a real feeling I had not experienced on a very low level beforehand.

Heather Bailey helps you learn tools in order to feel, to be seen, and to begin loving yourself and others in this experience we call earthly life. Thank you, Heather.

—Erika Barney

I really like that there are tiny action steps that feel doable. And not just one. Lots of suggestions gave me the chance to consider which one best suited me at the time.

I like that the stages are clearly laid out, with very simple, doable action steps for each one. It makes sense to have them in a progression from bottom to top of the body.

I really loved that she gave suggestions of actions for different groups and personality types, and what things might resonate with each group. It helped to see all kinds of options.

The UNdepressed Heart fills a need for young moms who are feeling overwhelmed and depressed, who need a simple way to lift their eyes and minds up to more light. I fit in this category, and as one of these moms, the tiny steps are things I can easily fit into my busy life, without feeling like they're impossible to do.

—Ann B.

The UNdepressed Heart has so many tools to help yourself and others to be at heart-level; loving people and supporting them where they are. I am so thankful Heather is authentic. She has put her research and wisdom into this book for others to climb out of depression and have tools to live a better life. I am getting extra copies to give to people I care about. A must-read to make this world a better place. Thank you, Heather, for making my world a better place.

My thank-you to Heather:

Thank you for sharing this book with me. I really enjoyed it. Not only are the tools in this book useful to help get out of depression or unhappy feelings, they are also life tools to make my world a better place. I have experienced depression before. Now I can refer back to this book to lift myself and others. I enjoyed your stories as well.

—Raquel Attar, Young Living Health and Wellness Coach

I really enjoyed reading *The Undepressed Heart*. It is a great book discussing the six stages of depression. Even though it is written with the young mother in mind, I believe it can be highly useful for any age or gender. There are clear and easy steps to help anyone dealing with setbacks in their lives, including anxiety, fear, worry, and grief. The insight to stumbling blocks was exceptionally written. I would definitely recommend it to a friend or family member who might be struggling with depression and looking for the road back to happiness.

—Elaine Blymiller

As I read *The UNdepressed Heart* by Heather Bailey, I was impressed by her depth of understanding of the way feelings work in the human body and how they affect our lives. She also writes with a style that's easy to read and understand. It was enjoyable.

In the stages of depression she defines, she not only gives the keys to assessing where a person is emotionally, she also gives tools that anyone can use to help a person move up and out of depression. In fact, the person experiencing depression can use it for themselves. The goal of getting to a higher level of feeling is not to just be undepressed, but to be at least in a state of happiness.

Happiness is often misunderstood. She lists some generally accepted myths about happiness that we need to get rid of. She lists ten stumbling blocks that can keep us from feeling happy and what we can do to eliminate them from our lives.

This book provides a very good recipe for finding and living a life of happiness and joy. And even though it is written for young mothers, the concepts can be used by anyone. I will be reading this book again to make the information more completely mine. I will also use these principles with people that I know and will recommend the book to others.

—Ken Jones

Reading *The UNdepressed Heart* was like having a one-on-one conversation with Heather Bailey herself. I truly felt my thoughts and feelings were being validated and understood. The Six Stages of Depression were reinforced throughout the book with deeper understanding each time. I was so inspired by Heather's suggestions that I actually got up and took my dog for a much-needed walk. I have moved on to the grandmommy stage with grown children and have several friends and family who need this book. If you want an exercise program for happiness, this is it. Thank you, Heather Bailey.

—Holly Dean

The UNdepressed Heart

A MOMMY'S GUIDE UP AND OUT OF DEPRESSION

HEATHER BAILEY

Copyright © 2021 Heather Bailey

ALL RIGHTS RESERVED

No part of this book may be translated, used, or reproduced in any form or by any means, in whole or in part, electronic or mechanical, including photocopying, recording, taping, or by any information storage or retrieval system without express written permission from the author or the publisher, except for the use in brief quotations within critical articles and reviews.

office@feelwelllivewell.com

www.feelwelllivewell.com

Limits of Liability and Disclaimer of Warranty:

The authors and/or publisher shall not be liable for your misuse of this material. The contents are strictly for informational and educational purposes only.

Warning—Disclaimer:

The purpose of this book is to educate and entertain. The authors and/or publisher do not guarantee that anyone following these techniques, suggestions, tips, ideas, or strategies will become successful. The author and/or publisher shall have neither liability nor responsibility to anyone with respect to any loss or damage caused, or alleged to be caused, directly or indirectly by the information contained in this book. Further, readers should be aware that Internet websites listed in this work may have changed or disappeared between when this work was written and when it is read.

Printed and bound in the United States of America

ISBN: 978-0-9987865-7-5

DEDICATION

I dedicate this book to the powerfully positive influences in my life:

To my ultrasupportive amazing husband, Eric, who cheers me on with every step. Without Eric, the Six Stages of Depression would not be known to the world today. Thank you, Eric, for being brave, bold, and sharing your genius with the world. I love creating this glorious life together!

Unconventionally, I thank myself for pushing through and getting this done! I am humbled to share this with the world of women who need this most today!

And I thank YOU for investing this time into yourself to learn, grow, take action, live from your heart again, and truly love your life!

Let's begin!

Dear Friend,

First of all, if you need help, please get it. You are too precious to be feeling so low. You are worth getting help, and you are worthy of feeling better. Yes, you. If necessary, make an appointment with a professional. If you feel so inclined, get some medication if you might need it. Seriously, you are totally worth it.

Please get all the help you need, because you are worth it (though you may not feel like it yet).

If you're feeling so low you don't want to even do that, read this book through to Stage 5, and then seek professional help of some kind.

There is hope for you, even if you don't see it yet. Your hope is just around the corner. Hope is as close as your next breath, so breathe it in.

Disclaimer: This book is not medical advice; this is happiness science. If you are on medication, always get your doctor's approval before lessening or quitting any medications you are currently taking. Please get all the medical or professional help you need; you are worth it (even if you may not feel like it yet).

Table of Contents

Could I Really Feel Happy Again?...1

Stage 1: Validate 5

Stage 2: Passive Nurturing..9

Stage 3: The Heart's Level 17

Get Above Heart-Level: Look Forward! 21

Stage 4: Ask for Help—Use Your Voice.......................................27

Stage 5: See the Good—Get Moving Again in Nature 39

Stage 6: Celebrate!..51

Moving Forward Again..65

Why Happiness? 75

Stumbling Blocks...89

Giving REAL Support 113

Understanding FAWPA 131

Grief and Guidance 143

Building Better Relationships..153

Letters of Love...165

You've Got This, Girl!..169

Acknowledgments 175

About the Author...176

COULD I REALLY FEEL HAPPY AGAIN?

I see you, girl, sitting there in the middle of your living room floor, head down, eyes covered, wishing you could just give up and cry and cry. You don't want to blame your kids or husband for your totally overwhelming life, because you know better, but it still dang hurts. It's so crazy hard sometimes. You wish you could do and be more, but everything is just so overwhelming, it's so hard to even try. So you just cry. Go ahead, cry it all out. I'll let you lean on my shoulder for a few.

It's not your fault that you're feeling this way. Unfortunately, so many people have given you terrible advice. On those days when you have zero motivation to even try to get out of bed, or you hurt so deeply you wish you could just numb your feelings, has anyone ever told you to just "get over it"? Do they ever tell you to just make lemonade, like "when life gives you lemons …," and it will all get better? (My husband just said, "That must be some pretty amazing lemonade if it eliminates depression!") Seriously, people don't know what to say, so they try to give you advice for a stage that you are not in. They just don't get it. If you have zero motivation and feel like totally giving up, the suggestion to just "go outside and exercise" is the *totally wrong advice*! That's not what you need yet!

Depression has been misunderstood for too long now. It's time to change how we support and love people through this extremely difficult time. My mission is to normalize the overcoming-depression conversation and give people REAL support. Too many of us experience depression and anxiety without any real help or support because most people around us have no clue where to even begin to give support.

It's really not your fault that you are feeling this low. What you are experiencing is totally valid, and it's OK to have feelings! It's OK to feel!

This is not your fault, but it is your responsibility. Do you still need to feel this way longer, or are you ready to start at least wanting to want to feel better?

What if there was a better way? What if you could live more connected to your heart every day? What if you spent your precious time doing things that matter most to you? What ignites your heart and passion? What energy sparks inside you when you get started on that one thing? Don't see it yet? You will. Trust me; it is possible.

I was down really low … depressed, but not really knowing it. I felt completely overwhelmed with my crazy life. I said things like, "I don't feel like myself. I just feel blah." You too? Have you ever felt that way? My heart was hurting; I was constantly frustrated by being the one in charge, but not really. I should have tried to keep things in order, but whoa, I was so overwhelmed with my own three kids that having other adults and their kids living there too was a lot to handle. I felt frustrated, overwhelmed, and out of control. I barely survived emotionally, and I dropped deep into depression. Ouch.

Hours … days … months passed, and I felt so worthless, so low. I wished I wasn't alive, it hurt so deep in my heart. I was apathetic and couldn't even get out of bed. Have you ever been there? I hope not, but if so, it's nearly indescribable, isn't it? I mean, who do you turn to and say all that to?

Really, all I had left were prayers and my dear husband, who loved me anyway.

Could I Really Feel Happy Again?

Is there a way up? Yes, of course; there always is. Even if you can't see it yet. What if I gave you a map, specific directions back up for when you drop below heart-level? You could know exactly what to do to move back up one stage, and then the next, and the next, until you feel happy and more like yourself again. Would that be helpful?

What if those dark thoughts of "I wish I wasn't alive" were simply a notification telling you what stage you're at? What if those notifications then show you exactly what you need to do to feel just a little bit better, thus quieting those dark thoughts? What if there was a better way of living? What if you could move up above heart-level, and then start moving upward and progressing in life? If so, would you do it?

The UNdepressed Heart

STAGE 1

VALIDATE

"Nothing is as empowering as real-world validation, even if it's for failure."
~ Steven Pressfield

Crushed. My heart and soul felt utterly crushed. I heard the words, but I couldn't believe they had been said about me. I felt so hopeless. I ran to my room, fell into my pillow, and just sobbed. I cried so hard my whole body ached. I felt empty as the words ran through my mind again, "You're not worth having a relationship with." Those words pierced my heart like a thousand daggers, my heart bleeding tears from my eyes. I couldn't move. I couldn't will my body to move and get up if I'd wanted to … but I didn't want to. If I was such a horrible person that I deserved those words, then what was the point?

I had no energy left in my heart to care … about anything. How could those words come from someone I cared about? From someone I thought cared about me, or at least should care? Confused. Broken. Empty. I could only cry. If my husband or one of my children had needed me in that moment, I couldn't have willed my emotion-laden body to get up and act even if I tried. My mind raced. "Why would they say that? What did I ever do to deserve that?"

I sank deeper, realizing that gossipy message had spread to many others I thought cared for me too. No one stood up for me to deny it. No one tried to build me back up. The message just kept spreading.

Have you ever felt broken before? Crushed? Feeling like a planet's weight is crushing you and there's no way out?

In this deepest, darkest moment of my life, I no longer wished to live. It sucks, I know. This last and final disconnect was tearing my mind down to try and break me in this last and final way.

Complete darkness. The smallest bit of light came to my heart. My sweet angel child saw her broken mother, and she held me in her arms without a word. Her actions validated me, saying, "You are hurting. You are seen. You need love."

My crying calmed, and my five-year-old Ashley saw me start to come up just a little bit and sweetly asked, "Do you want to do something fun?" She somehow sensed I still couldn't move or get up, so Ashley bounced downstairs, grabbed a pile of our favorite books, came back upstairs and laid them next to me, saying, "Let's read together."

Her kindness reached my broken heart. I wasn't happy, but I felt less crushed. Still broken, but no longer utterly hopeless. (Just mostly hopeless.)

Depression hurts. Depression lies. The shameful, "should-ful" lying thoughts you think when you're depressed bring you down. These lies are expertly crafted for you to begin to believe, and they drag you down deeper and deeper. Can we agree there's an opposing force in this world trying to break our morale, hurt us, and bring us down one step at a time? When you agree with those lies mentally, it just digs your emotional hole deeper, darker, lonelier, until the hole caves in and you're crushed. Stuck. Hopeless.

No matter the reason, depression cuts deep. Depression crushes. Honestly, depression sucks. I wouldn't wish it upon my vilest enemy. It's the most confusing, hopeless, darkest hole a soul could fall into. The end.

Stage 1: Validate

Kidding.

There is a way out. If you know where you are at, you can take the next right step UP.

I see you've been broken before. I see the quiet tears in your eyes. You may be trying to hold it all together, but your soul aches with depths of sorrows only known to you. You may smile at the world, a happy façade, but inside you might feel broken, crushed, and barely capable of surviving another day.

Please know you are loved. Please know you are worth it. If you are deep in despair, high five yourself for reading this! There is hope. You can move up just one tiny step right now, just a little.

The pit of despair sucks, so let's make it just a little less sucky, OK?

Stage 1 depression is the lowest, suckiest, "hurts so deep I'm now numb" point we humans experience. Down deep, you're hurting so much that you just go numb so you won't feel it all. Completely hopeless and apathetic, you see other happy people and you probably despise them because jealousy lies and says, "Happiness is so far from your reality; you'll never feel that way."

You have no motivation, no hope, and zero willpower to do or care about anything. You could be Tony Robbins in Stage 1, and you'd still have zero motivation. You feel like a rock, heavy and motionless. Emotionally you've got nothing to draw upon to even want to get up. At the lowest point, you seriously couldn't force your body to move if you wanted to. Apathy reigns in this realm. The thought "I don't care" is a constant, especially whenever something comes to mind that you could or "should" do.

And seriously, down here *you don't want to feel better*. If someone comes to you and advises you to "just get over it" or "just go exercise," you just want to punch them in the face! You don't, of course, but they are so annoying you wish they'd go away and leave you alone. You have ZERO motivation, so you don't have motivation to even WANT to feel better. Because in Stage 1, you don't want to feel better!

"Wow, Heather, if I don't want to feel better, what do I do then?"

The only thing to do in this sucky place is to ... validate.

Why? Validation gets your mind back on board, and suddenly you do care about something. Even if you just care that you're depressed and it feels crappy, you at least care that you're feeling crappy. Does that make sense?

Now play along with me. Stomp your feet and declare out loud, "Depression sucks!" Seriously, get up and stomp those feet on the ground and declare, "This feels crappy!" "I feel_____, and that feels yucky!" "This feeling sucks!"

With our kids, we have them say, "I feel disappointed, and that feels yucky!" or "I feel sad, and that feels poopy!" I dare you to say, "I feel poopy" and not smile. It's silly, so it really works well with kids.

Back to you. Validation reconnects you to your body. Stomping your feet "grounds" you. Validation gives you a foundation to build yourself back up. You may now begin to feel again.

Do it now!

Tiny action

- Stomp your feet and validate how you are feeling. "I feel _____, and that feels _____!"

Repeat this multiple times until you feel understood and validated. Now hug yourself and say, "I can handle this!" "I've got this!"

STAGE 2
PASSIVE NURTURING

"Self-care is never a selfish act—it is simply good stewardship of the only gift I have."
~ Parker Palmer

"Yes, I realize I am in stage two, but how am I supposed to care for myself when I can barely even take care of my kids?" In a stroke of brilliance I thought, "What if roles were switched? What if my kids cared for me for a few?" My sweet seven-year-old Ashley was totally on board! She turned on relaxing spa music, dimmed the lights, and set out to give me a "spa hour." My nails being painted, I lay on the ground with arms outstretched, and I closed my eyes. (Hopefully my other four children were not making too big a mess—I guess I could still hear if anything went wrong!) Nails painted, hair brushed, then came massage time! All the children gathered for mommy massage time. Each one massaged my back, arm, or leg, and it was a glorious five minutes. Hey, if it's fun and everyone else is doing it, kids will do just about anything!

When you are in Stage 2, it is critical to give yourself some passive nurturing. You're not quite ready yet to get up and actually do anything, but you can do something passive to at least bring a little smile to your face. Maybe watch a funny YouTube video, read a book you can easily enjoy, or listen to your favorite podcast. Sit down and passively do something to bring a tiny smile to your face.

I get it, this can sometimes be the most difficult thing to do. When you are a mommy and have no clue when the next 30 seconds to yourself might be, how are you supposed to take time to care for yourself?

You may say, "How do I nurture myself when I can barely even take care of my kids?" Here's the deal: lift yourself up a little, just to that next step, and then taking care of your kids will be much easier (trust me on this).

There is a glimmer of hope.

Everything is much easier to handle when you are above heart-level. Focus on that next step, and you'll begin to feel like you could handle anything that comes your way, because seriously, you can handle anything that may come. You are strong, amazing, and yes, beautiful.

Beauty shines through your eyes when your heart is connected to you. You are an amazing, beautiful, confident woman. Even if you can't see it yet, it's there within you. How do I know? Because I see you. I know your heart, and I know you are an amazing mother, loving, confident, powerful, kind, and gentle. Yes, you so can do this!

I get it, anything further than the next step in front of you seems ridiculous and unachievable, even unfathomable—without fathom. So start to emotionally lift yourself up just a little.

Focus on your next step. Honestly, if a beautiful, clean, orderly home filled with happy children and a totally supportive husband seems unreal and laughable, then that's not your *next* step. Simply focus on filling yourself with nurturing care.

At this stage, you're barely beginning to feel and see a glimmer of hope. Before, you didn't want to feel better, but now you "want to want to feel better." Does that make sense? You wish you wanted to feel better, but you still have super-low motivation to do anything

Stage 2: Passive Nurturing

about it. Now is the time to fill yourself with as much passive loving care as you possibly can.

Passive nurturing ideas

- Receive a "mommy massage"
- Watch a funny video
- Read a favorite book
- Take a warm bath or shower
- Listen to favorite music
- Order in favorite food
- Enjoy some chocolate (maybe dark, if you like that)
- Receive a hug or cuddles (I call it "holding")
- Listen to a meditation track/spa music

These next suggestions are a little more active if you are slightly higher within Stage 2.

Slightly active nurturing ideas

- Bounce on an exercise ball
- Bounce on a mini trampoline
- Light a favorite candle/diffuse a favorite essential oil
- Spend time with someone you care about
- Message or maybe FaceTime a friend
- Go outside and gaze at the stars (only if it's night, ha)

Passive nurturing means you don't move; you sit there and do something that lifts you a little and gives you a tiny smile. It could also mean you have zero mental resistance toward making a small positive movement, like getting up to get something. If it's easy and convenient, you're more likely to say yes to doing it when you need passive nurturing. In Stage 2, motivation levels aren't high enough to convince your body to move very much, but you can lift your spirit a little with passive nourishment.

Five Love Languages nurturing ideas

In this Passive Nurture stage, some of the best nurturing you can give yourself is through your dominant love language. Dr. Gary Chapman shared his brilliance with the world by revealing these five love languages:

- Loving touch
- Words of affirmation
- Acts of service
- Quality time
- Gifts

Here are more passive nurture ideas within the categories of the five love languages:

Loving Touch
- Foot, hand, arm, or a full-body massage (my favorite is an amazing head massage)
- Holding hands
- Being lovingly held in someone's arms
- Heart-to-heart hug—this is very powerful!
- Wiping away your tears

Stage 2: Passive Nurturing

- Soak in a warm/hot bath (this gently holds and warms your entire body)

Words of Affirmation
- Receive compliments from yourself or others
- Read a positive, loving note written for you
- Have someone read your favorite book to you
- Listen to an affirming meditation
- Listen to an uplifting podcast
- Read this book that tells you how amazing you truly are!

Acts of Service
- Order take-out delivered. Dinner is prepared and brought to you!
- Have somebody come and clean your home for an hour (paid, or as a service)
- Persuade someone to clean the room you're in
- Take a shower and get dressed
- Brush your hair
- Do your nails/get them done
- Ask someone (even yourself) to create or bring you a healthy treat

Quality Time
- This could also include any of the loving touch ideas
- If you enjoy reading together, do that!
- Play a game: board game, talking game, video game … play something fun with someone close to you
- Watch a movie or fun YouTube videos together
- Look up funny memes
- Eat delicious food together
- Do something passively nurturing with someone who cares about you

Gifts
- Give yourself a gift or lovingly persuade someone to offer you something that might bring a smile to your face
- Order food delivery
- Order an inexpensive gift for yourself
- Make yourself a healthy treat
- What do you like? Clothes, books, treats, shoes, a love note, flowers, makeup, new kitchen tools, new art supplies ... (Don't go overboard on this one: make sure your nurturing doesn't solely rely on buying something for yourself; only use this occasionally)
- What lights you up?

Remember, passive nurturing is doing something that puts a little smile on your face. At this stage, it must be passive.

Here's one more idea, and this might work really well if you have little girls: ask them to play "salon" or "spa day" with you. Have them give you a massage, put lotion on your hands and feet, paint your nails (if you dare!), gently brush your hair, feed you grapes, or better yet, chocolate. Maybe even "tip" them with something they like (reading with you, snuggles in a warm blanket, or, dare I say it, candy or a favorite treat—or maybe even a dollar—kids love spending power). Try it once and tell me how it goes! It might only end up being a five-minute massage, but you may end up feeling a little pampered in the process.

Why passive nurturing?

At this stage you're not ready to do anything that requires you to move your body. Positive energy and motivation come from the heart. In Stage 2 you're not quite up to heart-level yet.

Stage 2: Passive Nurturing

Stage 1 is where you've got to first convince the mind to be on your side. (Hint: You are not your mind. The mind is like a computer—running all the programs it's been trained to run. Its main job is to keep you alive.)

Stage 2: You need to feel nurtured, loved, and taken care of.

Stage 3: You must reconnect at your heart-level. Your heart and higher self can then convince your body to move where you want it to go.

When you fill yourself with passive nourishment, you finally realize someone does care about you: you care about you! You feel nurtured because you've been caring for yourself! Once you are filled with that care and nourishment, you are ready to move up to the next step.

Tiny action

- Passively care for yourself. Fill yourself with nurturing.

- Pick one passive nurturing idea and do it now.

Now give yourself another hug and say, "I can handle this!" "I've got this!"

The UNdepressed Heart

STAGE 3

THE HEART'S LEVEL

"Your Heartline is your Lifeline."
~ Heather Bailey

"I've given this all I've got!"
"Yes, but you can still give more."

My husband and I were bold enough to enroll in a self-mastery boot camp. We felt physically exhausted, mentally stretched, sunburned, and emotionally drained, but then we arrived at camp.

This camp was designed to test you beyond what you thought you could handle, stretch you beyond what you thought possible, and grow you more than you ever imagined. It pushed us mentally, physically, emotionally, and greatly tested our endurance. But then came the biggest test of all: it tested the strength of our hearts.

How much negativity could we handle and still stay strong? The masters of wisdom filed us students (of hopeful wisdom) into a large rectangular room. Immediately they split us up into groups of four: Eric followed one group, and I went to the opposite end of the room. They told us the best way through this was to remain in our hearts.

After a quick safety briefing, it was my turn in the "hot seat." I stepped up, and my group leader then faced me and yelled, accused, and bad-mouthed me to my face. She attempted to tear down my mind and heart verbally in every way: using sarcastic comments, lies, questions of doubt; stirring up anger, frustration, and telling me all the reasons why I wasn't good enough.

Have you ever felt like that? Have you ever had voices in your head tearing you down? It hurts, doesn't it? Especially if you start listening and agreeing with those destructive voices.

The pressure was on. Students began to believe the negative lies (because these negative thoughts were already in their heads before this even began). They just wished the destructive words would stop. People all around the room began to give up. The intense negativity was just too much.

Do you ever feel like your life is too much for you to handle? It cuts deep, right? It's truly hard, especially when you are below heart-level.

Accusations and insults were yelled in my face. She threw every verbal assault possible my way, yet my heart was never more filled with love than at that moment. I strongly felt compassion and love. How? Is it possible to still feel love with someone yelling at you?

I remained strong because I didn't let those accusations and destructive words get to my head.

I immediately immersed myself in my heart. I focused my thoughts on anyone I had ever judged, everyone this person in front of me represented. In my mind, I sincerely asked my accusers, "Will you please forgive me? Please forgive me for wrongly judging you. Please forgive me for being distant and ignoring you. Forgive me, please."

My heart filled with compassion; my eyes dotted with tears of sincere love. My acting "accuser" had difficulty continuing to throw destructive words at me; the intensity lessened. She later said the

Stage 3: The Heart's Level

feeling of love emanating from my heart made it really difficult to continue to insult me or tear me down.

That day, my husband and I didn't give up under those circumstances (unlike so many others) because we remained in our hearts. Even with someone attempting to negatively tear us down, we remained in our hearts. Eric's accuser later commented, "I couldn't tear him down. Eric has a lot of heart."

How did we remain in our hearts? Eric recognized the lies being thrown in his face as not true, and he mentally sent back light and love. I personally focused on sincerely asking for forgiveness. I imagined all the people I'd ever wrongly judged (including the "negative" person in my face), and I sincerely, humbly asked them to please forgive me.

Even you, please forgive me for judging. Please forgive me for delaying writing this book because I feared people strongly disliking me or saying it's a waste of time. Please forgive me. I am writing this now for your benefit because I love you. I know how deeply it hurts to be in the lowest stages of depression, and I wish to throw out a "heartline" to you. You can do this, my friend. You are amazing. I believe you are here for a reason, and you are worth every second I spend creating and sharing this book, just for you.

Please remember, a sincere plea of forgiveness will always put you back into your heart.

Try this now

1. Write a list of your family members.
2. Focus on one person you wish to feel more love toward (you know who it is).
3. Say their name out loud (if people are around, whispering works too), and sincerely ask them for forgiveness: "(Name), will you please forgive me?"

Let go of all old hurts and misunderstandings, and experience what it feels like to sincerely love that person who means so much to you. Immerse yourself in your heart: ask them for forgiveness for every mean thought, criticism, complaint, hurtful action, judgment cast, and anything else you've negatively thrown their way. Ask them, "Will you please forgive me?" The words "Will you please forgive me?" must leave your lips (even if in just a whisper) to be the most powerful and effective.

What if they are the ones in the wrong? "Why would I ask them for forgiveness? I didn't do anything wrong!" Why? Because you are too precious to continue hurting like this.

Asking for forgiveness HEALS YOU. It heals your heart.

Dr. Roland Phillips taught me years ago that "judgment = suffering." When you judge, you suffer. Pain happens, but suffering is optional. To suffer is to refuse to let go of the memory of the pain. I prefer not to suffer; I prefer to heal faster.

You've probably heard that holding grudges is like drinking poison and hoping the other person gets hurt, but it hurts you most. Think of it this way: wishing pain on another person only brings that pain closer to you. Do you really wish to continue hurting like this?

Be brave. Be bold. Take this simple action and ask for forgiveness.

Tiny action

- Ask one person for forgiveness, saying out loud, "Will you please forgive me?" (Say it to the actual person, or ask it out loud without them there. Do what you can do right now.)

Now that your heart is being healed through you asking for forgiveness, let's get your heart energy flowing again.

Hug yourself again and say, "I can handle this!" "I've got this!"

GET ABOVE HEART-LEVEL
LOOK FORWARD!

"Happiness is pretty simple. Someone to love. Something to do. Something to look forward to."
~ Rita Mae Brown

"She's totally replaced me. You don't even care about me anymore. Our daughter is more important to you than me now."

These secret thoughts ran through my husband's head over and over. He was slipping deep into depression, and I didn't even realize it.

I was so new to this motherhood thing. I felt like I had no idea what I was doing. After two weeks of intensive care, our baby was finally home with us! But I felt totally exhausted because #nosleep. That next month I literally had to sit up in bed to nurse my tiny 4 lb. preemie every couple of hours. I gave her everything I had day and night because I wanted her to thrive. Highly interrupted sleep went on for three months until we could coordinate side-lying nursing (a total sleep-saver for me!).

However, my husband saw my daughter there sleeping in bed near me as a literal replacement of him. Remember, this parenthood thing was totally new to him too. Not to mention the shock of her coming prematurely and being in the hospital's NICU those first two weeks.

To top it all off, at that time he was dealing with a lot of, in his words, "abandonment issues." Being adopted as an infant, he perceived his birth father and mother as having abandoned him, and this new perception of being replaced only aggravated it all. He saw our daughter next to me in bed as a literal replacement, and he never slept in the bed with me after that.

He worked ridiculously late-night shifts as a restaurant server. When he came home, he'd just fall asleep on the couch. He then waited until I woke up so he could "take his turn" sleeping in the bed. He would finish his few hours of sleep before doing the whole college and work thing again. We lived in this tiny home, so yes, sleeping arrangements became very interesting.

Until my baby was over three months old, I didn't even feel like a normal human being again. I was exhausted and felt totally new to this whole thing. I missed the fact that my husband was slipping deep into depression. I seriously didn't even realize that until years later when he told me more of his story and perspective.

He was slipping into depression ... but, there was one light for him. He decided to create the most magnificent dream birthday for me that he could imagine. (Yes, he is extremely sweet and amazing. I still almost can't believe he would do all that just for me!) He found pictures of everything he could do to give his "queen" the best birthday ever. He created a secret file (I never saw it) with pictures of all he wished to create during this wonderful time for us to spend together. He found pictures of the most magical experiences. For my 23rd birthday he envisioned a week-long Mexican Riviera cruise complete with parasailing, deep-sea diving, and ziplining through tropical rainforests. He wanted to give it all to me. The cost: $5,000.

Get Above Heart-Level: Look Forward!

Now, is $5,000 a lot or a little when you are college students earning around $2,000 a month? It's astronomical! It's almost unbelievable, but he intuitively knew our relationship would depend on investing that time and money into us being with each other, so he made it happen. He worked the longest shifts (as a restaurant server). Most weeks he'd work late night Friday and then a double shift Saturday (early morning until late at night). Week after week, he worked so hard, even combating extreme opposition from "well-meaning" family members who told him how foolish he was for spending so much money on our marriage. It was tough, but he got through it. Why would he do all that? He did it because he was determined to give me an experience we'd both remember forever, essentially saving our marriage.

He was looking forward to creating something he was very passionate about, and that brought him above heart-level. This gave him the energy, the heart-emotional energy (AKA motivation), to work so hard to bring us back together. It was so worth it, and I am forever grateful he lifted himself up by creating something to look forward to.

At Stage 3, you begin to want to feel better again. Since feeling happy is your next step, you begin to believe it is possible to feel happy again. The best way to do this is to look forward to something.

How about you? What is something you could look forward to creating? A favorite meal? (Eric loves creating "ultimate" meals.) Creating a work of art, like food, sculpture, painting, craft, quilting, or photography? Creating an enjoyable experience with someone you love?

What lights you up? Pick something, then start looking forward to creating and experiencing it.

Pro tip: In Stage 3, people sometimes feel like they don't have anything to look forward to. If you can't think of anything to look forward to, allow yourself to fantasize and dream about something amazing coming your way. If you experience it in your mind, it has the same effect as if it were real.

Get creative! Start planning. On your calendar, write the date you get to experience it. If it's written and scheduled, it's more real to your brain. If it's something you have resources and time for, do it today! Make a plan, and do it now!

Notebook prompt (you have complete permission to write here in this book):
- Possible ideas for things I can look forward to creating and experiencing are …
-
-
-
-
-
-
-
-
-

Pick something now! Schedule it and do it. This will light up your heart, reconnect you to yourself, and you will begin to feel happy again. If it's on the schedule, it's real to your brain. If it's a reality in the near future, you can start looking forward to it actually happening and maybe even start getting excited about it!

You'll notice as you look forward to this, your heart gets a spark of energy and happiness. That is the feeling of your heart's fire: your heart's energy is being sparked and turned back on because your true self/spirit reconnects more fully with your body. You start to feel happy and alive. You start feeling like "you" again.

Get Above Heart-Level: Look Forward!

The Heart's Fire

Have you ever felt like you had no energy, no heart to go toward something? But then you started a project and got superexcited about creating it. Suddenly, you had all this energy and motivation to create it, right?

When you are below heart-level and are trying to move back up and "restart" your heart's energy, there must be kindling for a spark to catch. Have you ever tried to start a fire with a spark, but there was nothing to catch on fire? Your heart is the same way; it must have that foundation and kindling before you try to "spark" excitement by looking forward to something. Asking someone in Stage 1 to get excited about something is like trying to spark a lighter without fuel in it (or light a campfire without kindling). It just doesn't work, right?

At the deepest stage, your validation sets the foundation. The passive nurturing begins to fill you up. You know you are cared for (even if just cared for by yourself). That passive care fills you up with the "kindling" to then prepare to start your "heart's fire" again. Now you just need a spark.

What sparks your heart? Well, at this stage, you aren't ready to fully be happy. NOW still doesn't feel so good, right? But if you look forward to something, then your brain can believe that it will feel good in the future. You begin to feel happy anticipating something new, good, and exciting.

Look forward to something fun, enjoyable, or look forward to creating something. If you love to plan things (like my husband does), plan a vacation for sometime in the next few months. Plan a fun meal you can create (Eric loves that too!). Plan a party (my friend LOVES planning fun themed parties). Plan a date night out with your husband and call a babysitter right now to schedule! Are you an artist? Plan a new painting or sculpture you are going to create. Plan something that sparks *your* excitement. When you are happiest, what do you love creating? Art? Food? Vacations? Parties? Read/write a book? Blog posts? Love notes? Gifts to give others? Baby blankets? Candles? Soap? Bath bombs? Favorite music playlists?

Anticipation of creativity and enjoyment will spark your heart. If it's already full of nurturing, then the heart's energy catches fire and you feel "alive" and like yourself again. You begin to feel happy.

Tiny action

Notebook prompts (you still have permission to write in this book):

- I look forward to creating …

- I am creating/experiencing it on this date:_____

Now love yourself. Give yourself a hug and say, "I can handle this!" "I've got this!"

STAGE 4
ASK FOR HELP—USE YOUR VOICE

"Healing takes time, and asking for help is a courageous step."
~ Mariska Hargitay

I'd never felt so miserable on a date before. Dinner was served. I barely talked ... hardly ate a bite. I just wanted to feel like me again. I confessed to my sweet husband how low I'd been feeling for months (you know, since my heart had been CRUSHED!). I functioned well enough to pretend to be happy and normal, but inside my heart lay dormant ... disconnected. Reaching for a lifeline, I used my voice and asked Eric to help me.

Fresh from high-level certification trainings, Eric combined fragments of tools and techniques and customized a breakthrough just for me. He validated my icky feelings. He walked me through my past to help me heal my perspectives. I received guidance, reassurance, and love. The best part? I felt like me again! For months I had merely existed, and now I felt truly connected to myself again. Happiness flowed through me. I began to look forward to creating tools to help others lift themselves up. I'd used my voice to ask for help, and I was ready to get moving again.

If you're in Stage 4, you are finally feeling connected to yourself again! Your "heart's fire" is on. You are feeling happy. You are actually starting to feel better. Congratulations! You are ready for the next step. It's time to use your voice and reach out for help. I know that may be uncomfortable, but you, my beautiful friend, are worth it. Write a list of everyone you can think of that you could ask for help in some way. (Yup, it's still OK to write ideas here in this book!)

- Mentor
- Sister
- Friend
- Husband
- Mother/Father
- Religious leader
- Minister
- Doctor
- Chiropractor
- Therapist (massage, mental/emotional therapy)
- B.E.S.T. practitioner
- Coach
- Mom's groups
- Supportive Facebook/online communities
- The person sitting right next to you

You must use your voice; this is vital in Stage 4. Using your voice to ask for help will reactivate your voice energy and lift you one stage higher. This also reconnects you to other people. Moving up to each stage represents reconnecting with key components and people in your life. The more connected you are, the happier you will become.

Let's continue helping you get happier. Now that you are starting to see the patterns of each stage, let's delve a little deeper.

Stage 4: Ask for Help—Use Your Voice

Questions of doubt designed to pull you down

"Doubt is not a pleasant mental state ..."
~ Voltaire

At each stage, the temptations, doubts, and thoughts placed in your mind are expertly crafted to pull you down one hurtful step at a time.

Questions of doubt:

Stage 6: "Why did this happen to me?" (Often blaming God for what happened or for allowing it to happen.)
Stage 5: "Why keep going?"
Stage 4: "Nobody can help me," or "Nobody will help me."
Stage 3: "Why bother trying? Why should I care? What's the point?" (This is the most disheartening question ever!!)
Stage 2: "Nobody cares," or "Nobody will help me."
Stage 1: "I don't care." "Nothing matters."

Now when these thoughts come into your mind, recognize them as a notification alerting you to exactly which stage you are in. Pay attention to your thoughts. When you know where you are, you will know exactly what you can do to lift yourself back UP!

To combat these, here are a few tips to help you keep moving upward. Answer these questions in the positive to move yourself back UP to that next level. Here are a few possible options:

Answers to lift you back UP:

Stage 6: *Why did this happen to me?*

- "Everything happens for my growth, experience, and becoming better. I can learn the lessons and grow and become stronger from all my experiences."

Stage 5: *Why keep going?*

- "My efforts make a difference. I add value to other people's lives. I am strong and committed. I am committed to reaching my full potential."

Stage 4: *Nobody can help me. Nobody will help me.*

- "Help is available to me. I am ready to ask for help. Multiple people are able and willing to help me. I am loved. I am cared about. I receive help simply by asking the right people for it."

Stage 3: *Why bother trying? What's the point?* (This is the most disheartening question ever!)

- Remember your "why" for moving forward. Tell yourself, "Every day I learn, grow, and progress. Simply by trying and doing, I become better every day."

Stage 2: *Nobody cares.*

- "I give myself nurturing and show that I care for myself. I am cared for. Lovingly nurturing myself lifts me higher."

Stage 1: *I don't care.*
- Validate by saying, "I feel_____ and that feels_____."
- Tell yourself, "I care about how I am feeling, therefore I do care."

Each stage has a choice: be dragged down, or move UP. The questions we ask and the answers we give either pull us down or lift us up. It's your choice. Personally, I like to choose moving UP.

Because these questions of doubt are expertly designed by opposing forces to pull you down, we must be extra vigilant and aware of our thoughts. Those doubts are meant to cause disconnect at each level. People experiencing depression feel that disconnection, and it feels like something is missing.

Disconnects

Have you ever tried to give someone a high five, and you both totally missed? Or have you ever tried to plug your phone in to charge, and it just doesn't register that your phone is plugged in? My husband's phone is wacko: sometimes it says it's charging, but then a few minutes later his phone turns off because the battery is completely empty! There's a disconnect somewhere.

Disconnection is a real phenomenon, even if it's invisible at times.

It's very important for you to understand the disconnects that occur as someone sinks deeper into depression. If you can see the patterns, you will know what to do when you or a loved one experiences this (and yes, this is way more common than most people realize).

Disconnects at each stage:

Stage 6: Disconnected from **God/the Divine.**—*Feel sincere gratitude and celebration.*

Stage 5: Disconnected from **nature and the world around you.**—*Get moving in nature.*

Stage 4: Disconnected from **other people.**—*Seek help and talk to other people; begin to feel heard and understood.*

Stage 3: Disconnected from **your heart**, your spirit/higher self. *You don't feel like yourself because you have literally disconnected from yourself.*—*Begin to look forward to something you will enjoy creating or doing.*

Stage 2: Disconnected from **your mind.**—*Self-nurture.*

Stage 1: Disconnected from **your body,** your feelings and emotions. No motivation to move or care for your body.—*Validate!*

Total disconnect: The next stage to drag you down is the literal physical separation from your body. If you get low in Stage 1, the temptation is for that final and permanent disconnect from your body. Combat those thoughts by saying, *"Thank you for sharing, but I choose to live!"*

These questions of doubt create more and more of a disconnect within you; they are designed to pull you lower one stage at a time. This is why it is critical to know and understand these patterns, so you can counter them and learn to lift yourself UP no matter what you are currently experiencing or feeling.

Stage 4: Ask for Help—Use Your Voice

In order to build yourself back up, you must reconnect at each level. That is what the tiny action steps in this book are all about! These actions help you reconnect with yourself, other people, nature, and God/the Divine. The more connected you are, the happier and more energized you will feel.

Build yourself back up again!

Stage 1: Reconnect to your body: *validate your feelings, emotions, and what you are experiencing.*

Stage 2: Reconnect to your mind: *self-nurture and show yourself you care.*

Stage 3: Reconnect to your heart and true self: *look forward to something you will enjoy.*

Stage 4: Reconnect to other people: *ask for help from caring people (this helps you feel heard and understood).*

Stage 5: Reconnect to nature: *get out and get moving in nature.*

Stage 6: Reconnect to God: *learn the lessons, feel sincere gratitude, and celebrate!*

It's interesting that in order to reconnect, you must build yourself from the bottom up, and at the same time it reactivates your body/spirit from the top down. In the lowest stages (felt from your stomach and intestines and down), you get your mind back on board through validating and nurturing. In the middle stages (felt from your diaphragm to the heart and chest area), you get your heart back into it. In the top stages (felt from the neck up to the top of your head), your body is then able and willing to move and progress again.

As you build yourself from the bottom up, it also reactivates you physically from the top down. Does that make sense? Mind, Heart, then Body. When you're deep in Stage 1 depression, If you try to just will your body to move, it doesn't work so well. You must first reconnect with your mind and heart to create emotional energy (AKA motivation) to then move your body and begin to make forward progress again.

Connections at each stage:

Stage 1: Feelings/emotions—Body
Stage 2: Mind
Stage 3: Heart
Stage 4: Other people
Stage 5: Nature
Stage 6: God/Divine

When you are fully connected at each of these stages, you feel happiness, joy, and you are no longer experiencing depression. Congratulations!

Take Action: Recognize where you are, and take the action listed for that stage in this book to help lift yourself higher!

Getting ready to ask for help

*"Ask for help, not because you are weak,
but because you want to remain strong."*
~ Les Brown

Stage 4: Ask for Help—Use Your Voice

Sneaking around the corner, Eric peeked out to see if I was sitting on the couch. He tiptoed quietly across the hall and into the bathroom. He'd come to associate being in my presence with the "mental daggers" I sent his way. (Ouch!)

He was still sleeping on the couch each night, and I would get out of bed early each morning with my first-born baby so he could "finish" his night's sleep in the bed. I was totally sleep deprived and not happy about our sleeping arrangements. Before I knew better, I sent these mental blaming and complaining daggers toward Eric as soon as he woke up. I didn't mean to, and I didn't know he was picking up on the energy of those thoughts (I used to believe the lie that thoughts don't matter much), but their effect was really damaging our relationship.

Luckily, the self-mastery world came to the rescue. I learned to release all my negative thoughts and pent-up emotions in a healthier way. I wrote them all down, destroyed the paper, and talked out loud to myself to get all those yucky thoughts and emotions out of me. That helped me release all that negativity. And guess what: Eric started to enjoy being with me again! (Imagine that!)

Dumping vs. talking

Now my husband and I know better. We always release our "emotions" before sharing our "feelings." What's the difference? Emotions are the physical processes that take place inside the body in response to different stimuli. Simply put, emotions are the energetic charge. On the flip side, feelings are how you actually feel about what is going on. For example, you may feel the emotion of anger, but the feeling underneath the anger might be "upset," "wronged," "disappointed," or "frustrated."

- Emotions come from the body (the energetic charge)

- Feelings come from the heart

> First clear your negative emotions (negatively charged energy), then share your feelings and concerns and seek possible solutions.

Always remember to process your emotions while alone. You never, never, NEVER want to "dump" your emotions onto another human being (e.g., "I hate that you ..." "You never ..." "Why do you always ...") because doing so is extremely toxic. You may feel better after "dumping," but the person you "dumped" on feels much worse. That really hurts your relationships.

Whenever you are emotionally charged, find somewhere to be alone (your room, the shower, your car, or out in nature). Cry, yell, scream, or throw a tantrum. Get some paper and write it all out. Get all that yucky, emotionally charged energy out of you. Only then may you share your feelings with someone who is ready and able to help you. Own up to your feelings and use phrases like, "I feel sad when ..." or "I feel it would be better for us to ..."

Allow the wave/surge of emotion to "roll on" and process through it, then discuss feelings with the person you need to make something better with. If you discuss problems during this negative emotional surge, it never goes well.

> Allow emotions to dissipate before trying to solve problems.

Whenever possible, get above heart-level first. You are able to listen with more understanding, seek possible solutions, and love unconditionally when connected with your heart.

Stage 4: Ask for Help—Use Your Voice

Resolving internal and external conflicts

Step 1: Release your negative emotions while alone.
Step 2: Ask permission before talking with someone about your feelings.
Step 3: Apologize and forgive.
Step 4: Seek possible solutions.

Always ask permission before sharing your feelings. You must make sure the other person is in a healthy mental-emotional state where they can listen and help you. For example, Eric and I always ask each other, "Are you in a place where you can help me right now?" If they are below heart-level, it's usually not a good time to talk with them. If they are above heart-level, they will usually say yes. If they give permission, then you may begin to express your feelings.

Avoid blaming and complaining. Simply express how things have caused you to feel or how you feel about certain things. Begin with "I feel …" (this allows you to take responsibility for your feelings and avoids placing blame on the other person). Go into this with the intention of finding a win-win situation.

Dump your emotions prior to this; get that out of the way, and then share your feelings with the intention of finding possible solutions.

You can do this!

Tiny action

- Write down two or three possible people you can reach out to for help.

- Release emotions (while alone!).

- Now go and ask permission. If it's yes, then ask them for help.

Get this done!
Self-hug time again! Say, "I can handle this!" "I've got this!"

The UNdepressed Heart

STAGE 5

SEE THE GOOD— GET MOVING AGAIN IN NATURE

"See the good in the world."
~ BYU TV

Clinging desperately to the mountainside, I looked up at my husband, thinking, "Am I going to survive this? How do we get off this mountain now?" I slipped on the ice patch and fell fast, grabbing onto the rocks on the side of the mountain. My fingers and arms were scraped and bleeding; thankfully I slowed to a stop before reaching the edge. Desperately trying to get a foothold, I called up to my husband, "What do I do now?" It was obvious I couldn't climb back up to him. He thought, "I can't just leave my wife hanging there to try and get down off this mountain by herself, but how the heck do I get down there safely? And then how do we find a new path down?" Bravely and lovingly, slowly, inch by inch he slid down to where I was. Together we were determined to find a new path back down to safety.

Exhausted, seeing his wife nearly fall off the mountain, and having zero tread on his tennis shoes (interesting hiking shoe choice, right?), slipping and making frustratingly slow progress, Eric began to doubt and wish to give up. I realized that if we both dropped below heart-level, we would have zero heart to even try to get off this mountain. So I did everything I knew of to stay very high mentally and emotionally. I sang and laughed. I noticed the gorgeous beauty of the mountainside. "I mean, look at all this snow. Our trail on the way up didn't have this much snow, but look, snow!" Inch by inch, we sloooowly got closer to another, safer path. I skipped along and smiled. I admired the beauty of the magnificent mountains surrounding us. I adored the waterfalls, flowers, and glorious views of the world below. I totally immersed myself in the vibrant energy of being out in nature.

When you are finally above heart-level, feeling connected to yourself and feeling happy, the best thing to do is get moving. Get up, get out, find some nature, and take a walk. Do something you love while being outside. Moving your body, especially out in nature, will help lift you UP to the next level. Connect to nature, and you are ready for the final step.

Do it now! Take a walk around your neighborhood—see the trees, the flowers, the plants, the blue sky. (Even NYC has small patches of visible sky!) See the mountains, the clouds, the sun, and feel the wind. If it's raining, take an umbrella. No matter the weather, immerse yourself in nature for at least five minutes.

Action 1: Put your shoes on (optional).
Action 2: Open your front door.
Action 3: Step outside.
Action 4: Walk outside for at least five minutes and focus on seeing nature.

Pro mommy tip: If it's too much hassle to get shoes and everything on your kids because you'll need to take them with you ... don't. Just open your front door and walk in circles in your front (or back) yard for five minutes. That way you're still close enough to hear/see your children, but you're still moving around outside. Make it work. Make it happen. Do it now.

Stage 5: See the Good—Get Moving Again in Nature

A small step in the right direction is always worth it.

The most important step is the first step. So take it now!

Heart-level living

Why am I so passionate and excited to talk to you about depression? Seems a little ironic, right? Excited about depression? It's because I see the power in knowing and identifying the patterns in a person's life. Once you can see it, you can change it. Once you understand the patterns, then you have the power of knowledge and action to change your state of being. Whenever you begin to feel icky or hear critical thoughts in your head, you can recognize which stage below heart-level you are at, remember the action step to lift yourself UP, and then do it!

My daily goal is to be above heart-level. Of course, the ultimate goal is to be totally reconnected at all levels, progressing, and feeling fulfilled, loved, valuable, and absolutely amazing! I find if I focus on being above heart-level, once I'm there, I naturally desire to keep moving up all the levels and making progress in my life. Once I dip down below heart-level, suddenly everything feels icky, nobody is good enough (including me), and I start getting frustrated, annoyed, critical, and just not nice (even if it's mildly not nice, it still doesn't feel good).

Heart-level is where I am living from my more true/authentic self because I am connected with my spiritual being. Take away your heart's energy, that heart-level connection, and life gets more difficult. You may begin to say things like, "I don't feel like myself," or "I just don't feel happy." You might have a running commentary going on in your head about how you can't stand what your husband did, or that your kids are so messy, or "Why can't people clean up after themselves?

They are such slobs!" or "Why do I have to do everything myself?" and "Why won't anybody listen?" And the blah-blah continues on and on … until you do something to lift yourself back up above heart-level to quiet those voices of criticism, blame, and complaining.

I'm a total self-mastery enthusiast, how about you? Once while at a self-mastery class I heard someone say, "Don't blame—to blame is to be-lame." It's true, don't b-lame! This is exactly why my focus is always on being above heart-level. Yes, I get frustrated at stupid things. When that voice of criticism starts running through my head, that's a telltale sign that I've slipped below heart-level. Since I know exactly which stage I'm in, I use the proper action to lift myself back UP.

It's not always easy—the deeper down in the stages I fall and the harder I crash, the longer it may take to build myself back up, but I know I can do it. Depression that could have lasted months or years now lasts minutes, hours, and if really deep, maybe days. Do you see the difference? Do you see the power you now have? Months and years of experiencing depression can instead turn into days and hours—simply because you now have the tools, the knowledge and wisdom to know EXACTLY where you are and EXACTLY what to do to lift yourself back UP.

No more blaming. No more waiting for other people to "care" about you. You care about you. You build yourself back up, one tiny step at a time, and you are now in total control of your life and how you respond. You can focus on being above heart-level. I suggest you make being above heart-level your daily goal. If you're still deep down, don't worry, you'll get there. Keep validating and giving yourself as much passive nurturing as you can, and then you will be ready to believe that being back up above heart-level truly is possible.

In order to stay above heart-level, you must understand the "counterfeits" that can start to try and drag you down.

Stage 5: See the Good—Get Moving Again in Nature

Counterfeits

Two kids ran and hid behind a boulder. They began to discuss their master plan. One said, "Let's just get some fake IDs, and it'll be easy." The other responded, "Is this really all worth it? I know we have to be 18 to buy it, but I think the fake IDs will cost more than the fish we want to buy." They wanted fake IDs just to buy fish from their local pet store!

Funny story, but isn't that true, though? In the end, being fake always costs more than being true and authentic. Giving in to counterfeits can be extremely detrimental. Counterfeits are costly, and it is crucial to understand the counterfeits that will try to tear you down.

What exactly do I mean? Each feeling/emotion has a counterfeit—an opposite or false imitation of its truth.

I totally fell into this trap when I was experiencing depression in Stages 1 and 2. I felt like, "Nobody cares about me." I don't like admitting this, but I would imagine myself falling down the stairs, breaking an arm or a leg, just so people would then "care" about me. The problem? Well, deep down I didn't actually wish to hurt myself. And the real problem? That isn't seeking care; that is seeking sympathy.

It's very tempting to believe that "nobody cares about me, therefore I will make them care." It may seem unbelievable that somebody could actually care, so you go after the counterfeit: sympathy. Why is this a problem?

1. As you saw, I wished to physically harm myself in order to get someone to "care" or show sympathy. That's not cool.
2. This could lead to chronic "victim mode," constantly seeking sympathy, yet never really feeling cared for.

What I really needed in Stages 1–2 was to validate and fill myself with passive nurturing, and then get back up to a level where I realized people did care about me.

If you can see the patterns, you can call them out for what they are: counterfeits and lies!

Stage 1 counterfeits and lies

"If I die, then I won't feel this numbness/pain anymore."

Total lie! Can I get a little spiritual for a second? We read in scriptures that the state in which we leave this life is the state of being we will be in the next life. Without a body for that space of time, it's much more difficult to repent and change. Dying does not solve any of your problems. It just ends your mortal progression, and it causes deep, deep hurt for the people you leave behind (yes, unfortunately I know exactly how that feels—too many people have been lost because of suicide, and it hurts … deeply). Please, my friend, choose to live. If you can just get back up above heart-level, you will see that. You will remember your purpose, your love and happiness. If you're not there yet, trust me, you will get there.

Stage 2 counterfeits and lies

"Nobody cares about me," or *"If I get hurt, then people will have to care."*

Bogus!!! First off, people and God totally care about you. You may feel empty and hurting and not see that, but there is always at least one person who cares about you. Your Maker will always love you and care about you. My friend, I care about you too. That's exactly why I am writing this, in hopes that this mother, who means so much to her family, her husband, her children, who means so much to this world, will read this, identify the patterns, and begin to lift herself UP. I hope she will see her purpose, reconnect with her soul and passions,

Stage 5: See the Good—Get Moving Again in Nature

and choose to live and become the best version of herself. I hope to reach your heart and let you feel how much I truly care about you. One day, I may even get to meet you, embrace you in a loving hug, and tell you how amazing you are. You've read this far, so I know you are a truly amazing, loving, wonderful woman.

Stage 3 counterfeits and lies

"I'll never be happy again."
That's so not true! The really cool thing about lies is this: opposing forces are expertly crafting thoughts to get you to move opposite the direction you wish to go. They aren't original, by the way; it's so predictable! Once you see the patterns, it's almost laughable, like, "Really, you used that yesterday! What makes you think I'm going to believe that bogus lie today?"

The exciting part about these lies is that all they do is tell you the exact opposite of the truth. For example, in Stage 3, you are just under the stage where you will begin to feel happy again. So what lie do they plant in your mind? "I'll never be happy again." That is the exact opposite of the truth because you are literally one step away from feeling happy again! Do you see it? The lies in your head are the exact opposite of your truth.

Do an exercise with me right now. Write down the top ten lies in your head. This is the exciting part: now turn those around to the opposite, and that's your truth today! To give those new truths more power, simply add an extra empowering statement to each of them.

Example lies:
- *"I'm not good enough."*
- *"I'll never feel happy."*
- *"Why bother trying?"*

The opposite of these and the real truth is:
- *"I am more than good enough because I am amazing."*
- *"I am so close to feeling truly happy."*
- *"I am naturally happy, and I love being me!"*
- *"Every day I learn, grow, and progress, and by trying I become better every day."*

Can I tell you a secret? I do this every single day. I write down the lies, and then I write down the positive opposite truths plus extra positivity. I tear up the old lies, throw them away, then read my new empowering statements out loud. This makes a huge difference.

Can I give you an extra super-ninja skill? I read the new empowering statements out loud in a "why" question form. Why? The brain will then go searching for the answers; it will start bringing evidence to your conscious mind as to why you are amazing, why you are happy, why you are fulfilled, loved, cared for, and fully nurtured. Does this make sense?

Don't believe those disempowering lies! Flip them on their head, and it will reveal the real truth to you. Seriously, try this!

Opposition is in all things. Opposing forces try to stop you, so they take everything that is true about you, flip it to its negative opposite, and then broadcast those thoughts to you. You'll always know what the truth is about yourself when you hear those thoughts saying things like, "You'll never make it. Blah-blah-blah," That usually means, "You're so close. You're going to make it. If you just continue forward, you will get there so soon!!!"

This exercise is quite effective even when I'm feeling low. It reminds me to look at the lies for what they are: blatant lies trying to tear me down. It reminds me that the opposite truth really is my truth and reality. It helps me lift myself back up above heart-level where life feels so much better, and I feel like I can handle my life.

Now let's explore Stage 4 counterfeits.

Stage 5: See the Good—Get Moving Again in Nature

Stage 4 counterfeits and lies

Have you ever heard these lies in your head before?:
- *"There's nobody I can turn to."*
- *"Nobody will listen to me."*
- *"Nobody understands me or what I'm going through."*
- *"Nobody can actually help me."*

At this stage, opposing forces are trying to stop you from reaching out and asking for help, which is exactly what you need to do in order to move up to the next stage, the next level of healing and feeling better.

Do me a favor. When you hear the lie "Nobody will help or listen to me," take that as a reminder of "Oh yeah, that means I need to reach out for help!" Immediately talk to your husband, your mom, best friend, or a professional. Schedule a B.E.S.T. treatment or some other type of therapy (you could even try massage therapy). Ask for some type of help, because using your voice to ask for help connects you to other people.

Stage 5 counterfeits and lies

"Am I doing too much?" or *"Am I enough?"*

This is where it gets interesting. Once you get up and start moving again, have you ever heard thoughts like, *"Am I doing too much?" "Am I too much?"* At this stage, the lie is proposed to you that, *"You're doing too much. Just relax, you're working too hard."* Or *"Wow, you are just too much: tone it down a little."* Or the closely related lie is, *"It doesn't matter what you do: you will never be enough."* The "too much–never enough" lie is expertly designed to get you to stop progressing! It tries to get you to stop being your awesome self, and it makes you feel that either the work you do is "never enough" or that what you are doing/being is just "too much." This immediately stops you from doing good, and it halts your positive progress.

You know that song from *The Greatest Showman*, "Never Enough"? It's so catchy that my children loved singing it all the time when the movie first came out. The only problem was that I didn't want that phrase getting stuck in our heads. The solution? I slightly changed the lyrics to be more empowering. Here are two new lyric options if you find that tune getting stuck in your head:

"Never, never, never too much. Never, never, never too much."

Or my personal favorite: "Never, never, never give up. Never, never, never give up."

It's true, you will never be too much as you are learning, growing, progressing, and becoming your best. Just see that phrase, "You're being/doing too much" for what it is, a lie. When you hear that, think "Yes! I'm so close to full connection: I'm so close to being joyful again!"

Whenever you hear, "You're not enough," always think and say, "I am more than enough because I am amazing!" Truth is, you are intrinsically valuable. You are a diamond: no matter how rough the edges or the amazing amounts of pressure you've been through, you are extremely valuable, and your worth as a person, as a woman, is priceless.

Stage 6 counterfeits and lies

"I'm not worthy," or *"I'm not worth it."*

The counterfeits and lies in this stage sound pretty similar to Stage 5's "too much/not enough," and those are, "I'm not worthy," or "I'm not worth it." The "I'll never be worthy no matter what I do" lie is designed to keep you from reconnecting to the Divine. It tries to get you to hide from God (as if that were possible anyway). The lie says, "If you're not worthy, then hide and don't approach God." The truth is, God loves us dearly, wishes the absolute best for us, and will help us every step of the way. He desires for us to become our very best, and if we reach out, connect, and ask for help, He will always be there for us.

The lies at this stage will do everything they can to stop you from this last, very important connection. If the lie can make you believe you are not worthy/worth it, then it will keep you stuck in this lighter stage of depression—but you are so close! Obliterating depression and reaching that joy in your life are as close as your next breath! Breathe in the joy.

Building you back up

Why does life get so difficult? Opposition is found in all things, but why? Without opposition, we would remain weak. Lack of resistance doesn't make us stronger. Lack of exercise doesn't build our muscles. Lack of opposition would actually create apathetic muscles and weak character. There must be opposition in all things to create resistance for us; we push against and overcome the resistance to become stronger. In that strength, we become better, and we can make the world amazing by adding value and blessing other people's lives.

When you can see these patterns for what they are, counterfeits and lies, then you can use them as notifications showing which stage you are in. Then you'll know exactly what you can do to move UP to the next stage.

The beauty of these patterns is this: the brain accepts and believes the next step is attainable. If you're in Stage 1, you believe you could feel again. When you are validated and understood, this creates the safety for you to be courageous and allow yourself to feel again.

Once you feel validated and have courage enough to feel, you begin to care about yourself.

You're not ready to move, so you passively receive nurturing, even if that's just watching a silly/funny video, or taking a warm bath.

Once you're filled with that self-care, you can emotionally breathe and believe happiness is possible. You look forward to something exciting, something you get to create or experience, and you begin to feel like yourself again, happy and more present.

From there, you believe you can reconnect with others, ask for help, and rebuild relationships. You feel more connected to the people you care about. You realize you are ready to get up and start moving, get out of the house, and take a walk and go somewhere. You begin to feel like you are moving and making progress in your life again.

Now you are ready to reconnect with the Divine.

Tiny action

- Go outside and start physically moving in nature

- See the good in the world around you

Now, wrap yourself in your loving arms and say, "I can handle this! I've got this!"

STAGE 6

CELEBRATE!

*"The more you celebrate your life,
the more there is in life to celebrate."
~ Oprah Winfrey*

"We're all set up!" Anticipating floods of people rushing through those doors, we saw the time: "9:00 a.m. Let's do this!" Doors opened … and … nobody walked in.

9:00 …
10:00 …
11:00 …

Nobody showed up. My husband and I looked at each other. Hmm … why are we here again? Fresh new business owners, we set up at a supposedly large expo in hopes of wowing people with our services to get some income flowing, but … crickets. You can't WOW crickets. We sat there twiddling our thumbs … and we were gonna be there for two days.

Granted, it was a large expo with hundreds of vendors, but nobody showed up. Maybe their marketing department didn't exist? (I know that's a blaming attitude, but that's where we were—I do know better now.) Um ... now what? The only people walking by were other vendors, but they were also there to make money (to at least cover the costs of being there!), not spend it ... so ... where are all the happy spending customers?

Nothing. Nobody. Now what?

I heard interesting words in our conversation repeat themselves. We had another partner who'd driven four hours to be there and at least hoped to make enough money to drive back home. Ha! I heard so much lack, disappointment, and discouragement. The focus was on what we didn't have, who wasn't coming, and complaints. Such a looooooong day.

After not wowing anybody and feeling defeated, we drove home.

We knew better, but I kept hearing, "But the reality is ...," followed by a list of complaints: total lack mode. We all know that what we think and feel (inner world) creates our results in reality (outer world).

How then could we, knowing this great truth, slip into only seeing and focusing on the negative? We are good people, and we teach and practice being grateful in all things. We attempted to stay positive the best we could, but we had no success.

My soul searched so deeply and eagerly for an answer.

As we tried to stay positive, in our language I kept hearing all the lack we had in our life: we were behind on paying rent, we needed gas money to get back home, we had little food at home, blah, blah, blah.

Basically, we needed to make money that weekend, but nobody showed up. I kept pointing this out, attempting to stop the "blah-blah," reminding ourselves to focus on the positive. I tried reminding us to focus on DO-wants, but sometimes we only saw the "reality" of not having enough in front of us.

Is that ever you? You know better, but "reality" is facing you with all these problems?

Stage 6: Celebrate!

My soul desired to know what one thing we could do to progress quickly and truly believe, nothing wavering, that we possess the creative power to *have, do,* and *be* everything we desire.

I focused, deeply desiring to know the answer.

My life's mission is to help lift others, shifting into abundance mode where we all can live joyfully as we so choose. I desired to know how to get there more simply. I knew there had to be something, so I searched and prayed.

Finding my answer

During the looooong hour drive home, I again heard in the conversation "lack" thinking. We knew better, but in our everyday language we talked about why we needed to make more money the next day.

I realized that others are mirrors to ourselves and everything we see in others is only a reflection of what we see in ourselves. So instead of calling out anyone specifically, I owned up to what I saw and heard. I turned to my husband and sincerely asked **the** question that I'd found in my heart.

"How can we always (constantly) be at a high level where we speak and live positively in order to attract/create abundance?"

Eric opened his mouth and inspiration from on high flowed through him, "I don't have the scientific evidence for this ..." I encouraged him to continue, and he said, "But when you celebrate, your brain produces hormones and emotions in the body. You then vibrate at the level where you attract abundance." He told me, "Write this down! This isn't coming from me. Write this down!" We scrambled for a pen and piece of paper, and I immediately wrote it down.

Wow! My heart deeply resonated with this truth. This was the most powerful "Ask and ye shall receive" moment of my life! Because I desired the answer so deeply and searched, meditated, and prayed, I received a most powerful answer.

Celebration night!

That night we chose to celebrate! If we had been in our old pattern, we would have gone home, seen little food, and grumbled that we were hungry and too tired to create anything good. However, in this new light of celebration in our life, we found a few dollars in our wallet and bought a couple of frozen pizzas for dinner. We found a few simple ingredients and created a delicious celebration cheesecake. We fully celebrated this new light in our life! It was simple, yet our choice to live in celebration transformed our entire mindset, thoughts, feelings, beliefs, and emotions into sincerely believing and feeling vibrantly abundant. The difference was the *choice* we made to celebrate.

Putting Celebration into Practice

Driving back to the expo the second day, it felt like we had entered into a new realm of reality. The billboards now said things like "Millions," "Be Creative," and "BEST BEST BEST!" I saw a Mother Teresa quote saying, "Peace begins with a smile," and another sign with the quote "The best way to predict your future is to create it."

We either had new eyes to see things we had not seen before, or I think literally overnight at least one of the positive billboards had been put up just for us. We were jazzed up and on fire—we were celebrating life.

We got to the expo, and it felt different. Next to our booth were bright balloons and upbeat music playing. The day was warmer and

Stage 6: Celebrate!

the sun was shining brightly. A cute little girl helped another vendor by walking around and enticing everyone with deliciously beautiful treats. This brought all of us smiles. Even the lady across from us (who had not smiled at all the previous day) was smiling because of the service this little girl gave the treat lady whom she barely knew. It was a celebration day!

Hardly any customers showed up this day either, but we celebrated that. We found little things to celebrate. We had found our key to staying at a high vibration, and we weren't going to let anything get us down. If something tried to pull us down, we celebrated that. Just by simply stating we would celebrate, our bodies and souls were filled with thoughts and emotions of celebration, and we immediately shifted back into feeling joyful. Our joy tanks were full and overflowing to those around us. If past negative patterns tried to take hold, we said, "Let's celebrate that," and they dissipated instantly. This is the fastest tool I've ever seen for this: It works at the speed of light *because it is light!* Celebration *is* light.

Take a moment and think of a time when you were truly celebrating: think of the feelings you felt, the loved ones you saw, the thoughts you held, and the emotions you experienced. Can you imagine having those thoughts and feelings more of the time? You can! The truth is you can.

Choose to celebrate every moment of every day, and this joy will fill you so completely that your life may transform miraculously into exactly what your heart desires. If the negative tries to slip in, simply state, "I choose to celebrate that," and immediately you will shine that bright light of celebration onto that negative darkness, and it is no longer there.

Darkness is an illusion—it is just a lack of light. If you turn on the light, no darkness can be there. Choose to turn on the light of celebration constantly in your life, and you will see miracles appear because miracles are a manifestation of light!

Receiving more after pondering new ideas

As I pondered more, I realized Christ's teachings are full of this truth. (Of course they would be, because He is the source of light and life.) Do you remember the parable of the prodigal son? When the son came home after spending his share of his father's riches (this son's entire inheritance), what did the father do? Did he mourn his loss? Did he reject or chastise his son? No, *he celebrated!* He caused a celebration to be held throughout his entire household in his son's honor. He celebrated his son coming back home to him and reconnecting.

They celebrated and surrounded themselves with an abundance of food, family, friends, and feelings and emotions of love, joy, peace, abundance, and celebration. Their hearts were filled with joy and exceeding gladness because they chose to celebrate!

The celebration did not restore the money lost, but it did help them reconnect and look forward to new possible solutions. The son learned many difficult lessons, yet he reconnected, celebrated, and began to build his life back up again. Despite difficulties and imperfections, we can all learn to build our lives back up.

My father once said when we create something in our lives, the opposing darkness inside us dis-creates it at the same time. In other words, the ratio of light to darkness inside us is how much progression toward our dreams and desires we see. If you hold a 50-50 ratio of light to darkness, there is basically no progression. 60-40 = slow progress. 70-30 is a little faster, and 80-20 is feeling pretty awesome. 90-10 is realizing your dreams quite fast, and with 100-0, your progress is at the speed of light because your whole being is radiating only light! You literally are light! When there is zero darkness, there is only light.

How do we then rid ourselves of the darkness and fill ourselves with light? The fastest way I have found is to radiate light and celebration!

Stage 6: Celebrate!

Celebration = sincere gratitude. Celebration is the highest form of gratitude. The Scriptures and all master teachers teach us to be grateful *for* and *in* ALL things because everything comes together for our good. Be grateful for the good, the trials, hardships, and afflictions because it all comes together for your good, experience, and progression. Everything in this life serves you, so be truly grateful. Celebrate and learn the lessons quickly to progress and reach higher levels quicker.

However, sometimes it is difficult to truly feel gratitude when your heart is disconnected. Depression = lack of joy. Depression is an illusion, just like darkness is an illusion. (Even so, it can still be painful.) When you add light, the dark doesn't exist. Depression is a lack of connection, and unhappiness is a disconnect from your true self. When you add the light of celebration, depression doesn't and can't exist in that same space of celebration.

Remember, happiness is your natural state of being. If part of you does not feel gratitude, but you express it anyway, you may feel a little better. How do you sincerely feel and believe that gratitude? Fill it with celebration! Celebrate everything in your life, because it all comes together for your good!!

> Remember, you are really only ready for this step when you are in the higher stages. If you try this at Stage 1 when you don't want to feel better, then it won't be very effective. You aren't quite ready for that yet. Stage 6 is the perfect place to use sincere celebration to fully reconnect.

Celebrate. Do what you love. Look forward to something you enjoy. Think of something that puts a smile on your face.

At the highest level, you are ready to reconnect with God/the Divine through sincere gratitude and celebration. When you learn the lessons from your experiences, you can celebrate this new wisdom in your life.

Learn the lesson

This life is about progression and becoming better. In order to positively progress, we have many lessons to learn. My favorite part is that we receive blessings when we humbly learn.

Blessings from learning:

1. Happiness
2. Loving what we learn
3. Learning more of what we love
4. Progress leads to happiness
5. Satisfaction comes when we challenge ourselves
6. Deep desire and ability to learn more
7. Gain knowledge to benefit self and others
8. Learning more enables greater service, love, compassion, and understanding
9. Everything we learn on our journey will help us with what is to come. (Seek direction in what to learn: the Lord knows you and what you will need later on.)
10. Become better and love and serve others more
11. Stability, peace, and knowing you can handle life because you can always learn the lessons

Happiness and joy come when we humbly learn, do good, and become our best.

One great lesson we all need to learn is to heal our perspectives. Heal your perspectives, heal your life. What do I mean? What is the meaning you have given to your past experiences? Did you view these things as happening to harm you, or as helping you grow and

Stage 6: Celebrate!

learn? I believe we are all on this earth for a reason. One main reason is to learn, grow, progress, and become the best we can. When we strive to do and become our best, God will sort out the rest.

How do we heal perspectives? B.E.S.T. helps a lot here. It literally updates your brain so you are no longer "reactive" to things in your life, both past and present.

Dr. M. T. Morter Jr. forever changed the world with his 40+ years devoted to clinical and scientific development of the Bio-Energetic-Synchronization-Technique (B.E.S.T. for short). This is the most powerful physical-mental-emotional healing tool I've ever experienced. My husband and I have healed so much in our lives using B.E.S.T.

Here's a basic demo for you to experience the power of B.E.S.T. right now.

Powerful B.E.S.T. demo:

- Let's experiment: think of something you experience that really stresses you when you think about it.
- What is the name of the emotion you are feeling? _____ (If it's "stress," write down the exact emotion you are feeling because of that stress, such as frustration, anger, worry, etc.)
- On a scale of 1–10, how intense is this emotion/feeling? (write it down!)
  1 - 2 - 3 - 4 - 5 - 6 - 7 - 8 - 9 - 10
- Now when you think of that experience, can you feel that intense emotion just by thinking about it? (If not, think of another emotionally intense example. If yes, proceed.)
- This is the demo part: put the middle finger of your right hand on your forehead, and the index finger of your left hand on your forehead, lightly touching just above your eyes.

- While holding these touchpoints, hold your breath, close your eyes, and repeat over and over in your mind, "Heart-Level #4, Heart-Level #4" (positive words and numbers have specific vibrations that can transform emotional energy into being more supportive to you).
- Now take a deep breath in, and let it all out through your mouth.
- Think back to the experience you wrote down. How does it feel now?
- Did the emotion lessen? Or maybe it's a completely neutral feeling now when you think about that experience?

If you can feel the difference, write that down! _____ _____ (Maybe even message me on Instagram @EverBeBetter and share your experience with me! I'd love to celebrate your wins with you!)

Isn't that amazing? You can now think of the experience without the stressful feeling accompanying it. By updating your brain to be more supportive of what you really desire, you no longer feel those negative emotions when you think of that experience.

This is what I mean by "healing your perspectives." Now you can look back to that experience and begin to heal those perspectives by giving that experience a new feeling and meaning. Maybe you're even at a level where you can learn the lessons from that experience and become a better person because of it.

If you could change how you feel about your life's experiences, what would that allow you to do differently?

If that little demo was that powerful for you, imagine what a full professional B.E.S.T. treatment could do for you!

Stage 6: Celebrate!

Change your story

"Everything in our life happens for us, not against us."
~ Tony Robbins

What if we healed and changed the perspectives we had? What if we changed our "life's story" to be more supportive? What if we changed our limiting beliefs to more empowering beliefs? What if we changed the story we tell ourselves? What if our reality was only a perception, and if we changed that perception, our "reality" would change?

My husband and I could have grumbled, complained, blamed the expo people, and focused on the lack of money ... but we instead chose to celebrate, feeling light and full of love in our hearts. We learned the powerful lesson of celebration in that moment.

Isn't that what we are here for anyway, to learn, grow, progress, and become the best version of ourselves while here on earth? My goal is to become like Christ in as many ways as I can: humble, loving, serving, eye-single to the glory of God, meek, submissive, powerful, full of love ... and every other positive characteristic.

Tell yourself, "I am here to grow, learn, progress, and become the best ME. I am awesome! I am totally amazing! I get better and better every day!"

Bonus Tool. Change the story.
- Write the old story you had about your life. (This shows you what you don't want.)
- Write your new story about your life: explain only what you DO want!
- Read your new story out loud every day for seven days.
  (Bonus points: listen to a recording of yourself relating the new empowering story.)

Your past is just a perception of what happened. You gave it meaning. You can heal your perception of the past using B.E.S.T. and rewriting the story. You can give your past experiences a new meaning. You can learn the lessons the past has given you. The past is a gift. If you change your perception, you will find the golden nuggets of knowledge hidden in your past. When you are ready to learn the lesson, you will discover that gold. How did the past shape you? What gifts and wisdom are hidden for you to find?

When you forgive and learn the lesson, you receive wisdom for moving forward in your life. How many people have you heard about who've had an excruciating past, yet they say "I wouldn't change it for anything"? They learned valuable life-lessons from that most difficult time in their life. Wisdom gained is much more valuable than having lived an "easy" life.

Pro tip: Nobody's life is easy. Everybody has problems and challenges unique to them, and life gets really difficult for everyone. Nobody is an exception. No matter what resources people do or don't have, life is a challenge. Will you rise to the challenge? Will you rise UP and become stronger from the things life throws your way? Will you say, "I will become better. I know better, I do better, and I become better"? Will you take on life's challenge? Will you do it NOW? Will you forgive and heal your past, so you can move forward now in your most powerful self?

I challenge you to heal, forgive, and gather all the golden nuggets of wisdom, stories, and empowering tools you've gained from the past, and invest it into your future. I challenge you to forgive, heal, learn, grow, and become the best version of you. You are worth it. You deserve to live the best life imaginable, and it is so close for you! It is your reality! Abundance of all your heart's true desires are as close as your next breath. Breathe it in. I know you can do this, my friend. I believe in you. I see the greatness inside you. You are a

Stage 6: Celebrate!

worthy mother. You are an amazing daughter of God; He loves you and will be with you every step of the way. You so can do this! You've got this!

Tiny action

Notebook prompts (write in this book, permission granted!):

- I am happiest when …

- Things I enjoy most doing are …

- Something I can look forward to is …

- My secret hopes are …

- My heart desires …

- I am sincerely grateful because …

- A time I celebrated from my heart was …

- I love myself because …

- I celebrate today because …

Bonus Points. Create a list: "1000 reasons why I celebrate my life"

One more time, hug yourself and say, "I can handle this!" "I've got this!"

The UNdepressed Heart

MOVING FORWARD AGAIN

*"You need to have faith in yourself. Be brave and take risks.
You don't have to have it all figured out to move forward."*
~ Roy T. Bennett

Is it crazy that I'm so passionate about discussing overcoming depression? I mean, who gets excited talking about depression? Almost an oxymoron, right? But I'm so amazed because we have found very predictable patterns. Once you see them, it becomes so obvious as to where you are at, and you know exactly what you must do in order to lift yourself back up, one stage at a time.

I get so excited talking about this, because this is power! This puts power into your hands, and if you know where you are at, you can know exactly what to do. When you do it, you can lift yourself up no matter how deep you are, no matter how much you "don't want to change" or "don't care." Because really, deep down in your soul you do care. If you can show yourself that you care, then you can get yourself back UP.

This is huge; this could be a life changer for so many people! My heart goes out to those dear mothers who don't know where to go or who to turn to for help. They feel so overwhelmed with responsibilities of motherhood that they can't even imagine caring for themselves! My friend, there is hope. There is a way. There is no hole so deep that the arms and love of Christ can't reach down and help lift you up. Whether you know it yet or not, He deeply loves and cares for you, my friend. You must choose to live a better life. You so can do this.

You don't have to have "clinical depression" in order to make use of these stages and action steps. Actually, I don't make any distinction between "clinical" or grief-brought, criticism-reacted, low self-worth, tragedy, frustration, anger, or whatever-caused. Whatever the reason you are feeling depressed, you are feeling it, and you are worth lifting yourself back up above heart-level. When you're connected at that heart-level, the sun shines brighter, and you have hope, value, and purpose. Above heart-level, you naturally desire to change and improve. No matter what dropped you below heart-level, it doesn't matter anymore. What matters most is getting you reconnected with yourself at that heart-level. You can do it.

Whether it's a diagnosed depression, or you just haven't been "feeling like yourself" lately, the distinctions don't matter too much because Stage 1 is Stage 1. If you feel so low that all motivation is lost, you "don't care," and you "don't want to feel better," it doesn't matter what caused it. You are feeling crappy, and that feels crappy. No reasons needed. Your feelings are valid simply because you are feeling them. You are valid, and every emotion you experience is a valid emotion.

The reason I love talking about this so much is that the patterns are predictable and easy to use. Once you get used to evaluating which stage you are at, you can know exactly where you are the moment you drop below heart-level.

You begin to recognize your "notifications." For instance, when I start thinking critical thoughts against others, I realize, "Oh, I'm below heart-level right now." I immediately assess which stage I am at, and then I do the action step for that level. This lifts me back UP every time. My daily focus is being at least above heart-level. The better you understand the characteristics of the six stages, the easier it becomes to keep yourself above heart-level.

Advanced Notification Training

Let's get into your advanced notification training. Now that you know the patterns, let's deepen your understanding and get you set up for success every day.

How do you know which stage you are at?
1. You can listen to your thoughts.
2. You can recognize how you feel.
3. Advanced notification: Ask yourself, "Where in my body do I feel this depression?"

It's exciting to realize that our bodies are so amazing! Your body will actually notify you if you listen. Where you physically feel the depression is a great indicator of which stage you might be in.

Stage 1

If you're feeling your depression in the lower half of your body (below the navel), or just not feeling anything at all, you're probably in Stage 1. Accompanying feelings will be numb, apathetic, and thinking "I don't care."

Stage 2

When you feel it in your tummy/abdominal area, that indicates you're in Stage 2. You might also feel like "nobody cares," and it hurts so much you just want to curl up in a ball and protect that tummy area.

Stage 3, below heart-level

Feeling depression at or above the diaphragm indicates you are "breathing," yet you're still below heart-level. This is when you can emotionally "breathe" again. You feel stable, and you're not drowning in the depths of depression anymore. You can function fairly normally, yet you're not quite happy yet. The repeated thoughts at this point may include, "I'll never feel truly happy," "Why bother trying?" or "What's the point?"

Stage 3, above heart-level

Feeling happy! You may feel the depression (it may feel like resistance, restriction, or just a negative "haze" around the area) anywhere in your chest or shoulder areas. You feel happy again, yet you may still feel some resistance toward asking for help or moving forward.

Stage 4

You may feel resistance in the neck or vocal area. This could include tight neck muscles, a sore throat, lost voice, or even tension headaches from overly tight neck muscles. Remember, it's critical at this stage to use your voice and ask for help. This will help loosen the resistance and restriction around your vocal area.

Stage 5

Resistance in this stage may manifest itself as headaches (especially in the forehead area), upper-facial breakouts, difficulty/changes with eyesight, or migraines (if you've ever had one, you know it's different from a headache!). You may think, "Am I being/doing too much?" or "How do I keep going?" Remember, getting outside and physically moving shows yourself that you can keep going.

Stage 6

You're almost there! Possible resistance in this last stage could look like an itchy scalp, maybe hair loss, or a headache on the top of your head. It also could feel like cloudy thinking or a mental "fog." Or maybe you just have too much on your mind. You might think, "Why did this happen to me?" If you answer that in the positive, then that will help lift you UP. Learn the lessons, see the good, and feel gratitude. When you can do that, celebrate the total obliteration of that depression! Congratulations!!!

Paying attention to where you feel the depression can help you recognize which stage you are in. This is how my husband Eric quickly identifies which stage his clients are in. He asks them where they are physically feeling it, and he then verifies it with a question like, "You are feeling it in your stomach. ... Do you feel like nobody cares about you?" They say with surprised eyes, "How did you know?" (Bingo!) He double-verified which stage they were experiencing. He then has them do the action step for that stage, and then the next stage, and then the next. Before they leave his office, they are feeling happy and above heart-level again. I love hearing on a weekly basis stories of people going into his office feeling "down, depressed, or unhappy," and then they leave feeling happy and alive again because they are back up above heart-level. He understands the indicators for each stage, and it helps him quickly assist his clients in moving back up to healing and being happy again.

Indicators for the six stages

Frequent feelings for each level:

Stage 1: Don't want to feel better
Stage 2: Want to want to feel better
Stage 3: Want to feel better
Stage 4: Feeling better
Stage 5: Start to get moving
Stage 6: Moving forward again

You know you're completely out of the "depression pit" when you are making positive progress, feeling truly joyful, connected, and loving your life!

Happy is the person connected with herself at heart-level.

Joyful is the person totally connected with God, nature, others, and self.

- Happiness = Being connected with spirit/true self
- Joy = Being connected with God/the Divine

Happiness is living above heart-level. When you live and love from your heart, you feel happy. If you can just get above heart-level, get yourself up to Stage 3 and above, then happiness is so obtainable for you. It is so close!

Here's an extremely powerful tool I use every day to lift myself UP:

The Happiness Pose

Each stage has its own interesting body "protective" movements. While you are healing and progressing, you can realign with the positive of each stage. Use the Happiness Pose to build yourself from the bottom → UP.

Stage 1: You feel like you have no "foundation." This is when people just want to stay in bed a lot. They feel they have nothing to stand upon.

> Step 1: Open up your foundational energy by standing up, firmly planting your feet upon the ground, and having your feet face forward.

Stage 2: Everything hurts deeply, and you feel it in your tummy. You either cover the tummy area up (sometimes with "comfort foods" or a blanket) or curl your body up to protect that hurting area.

Step 2: Turn your tailbone out so that your back is upright and straight and your hips tip slightly forward. This opens up your core energy.

Stage 3: Shoulders slump forward to cover and protect your heart. Your hands may tighten into fists (further closing off the heart).

Step 3: Pull your shoulders back and push your chest out, and relax your hands by your side to open up the heart energy again. (Open hands indicate an open heart.)

Stage 4: Head tipped down to protect your "voice."

Step 4: Tilt your chin up and smile. This opens up the vocal energy and connects you with other people (smiles are a way we connect with people and show them we care).

Stage 5: Eyes look downward to disconnect from the world and to look down into inner emotions.

Step 5: Eyes looking upward reconnects you with the good in this world.

Stage 6: Thoughts may be disempowering.

Step 6: Think celebrational affirmations to reconnect with God/the Divine.

Let's do this now! Stand up and do this!
Create your foundation, and build yourself UP!

Happiness Pose:

1: Plant your feet firmly, facing forward.
2: Put your tailbone out, hips tilting forward, and back straight.
3: Roll your shoulders back, and relax your hands by your side.
4: Bring your chin up and smile!
5: Lift your eyes to look upward!
6: Say, "I celebrate everything good in life."

Hold this pose for 60 seconds, repeating over and over in your mind, "I celebrate everything good in life."

I challenge you to do this for the next seven days (starting today!). See what a difference this makes in your life. Message me once you do this (Facebook: Heather Bailey, or Instagram: @EverBeBetter), and share what difference this made for you. I'd love to celebrate your progress with you!

We've got this

These are the patterns, girl! It just is. Opposing forces are expertly crafting designs to bring you down one level at a time. On the bright side, positive forces reach down their hands to help lift you UP every day. The direction you go is your choice. This is where free agency comes in for all. You get to choose which voice you listen to. Which thoughts will you believe? Down, or UP? It's your choice. This is your life.

Please remember to always give yourself time and space to heal. You are worth it. Life will still be up and down, but when you apply

Moving Forward Again

the wisdom of the six stages, get ready for your ups to be higher and longer, and your downs to be shorter in length. Life is just like a heartbeat: it has ups and downs, but it keeps moving back up.

> Remember this: You will still feel a huge array of emotions throughout your life, but you don't have to get stuck at the bottom anymore.

Now you know exactly what to do to lift yourself back UP one stage at a time. You can do this every time.

Tiny action

- Ask yourself, "Where in my body am I feeling the depression/resistance?"

- Take the appropriate action to lift yourself UP a little higher.

- Hold the Happiness Pose for 60 seconds.

  Give yourself a high five and say, "I've got this!"

The UNdepressed Heart

WHY HAPPINESS?

"Happiness is letting go of what you think your life is supposed to look like and celebrating it for everything that it is."
~ Mandy Hale

"When you hear a knock on the door, do you panic and try to quickly tidy up? Or do you feel calm and happy?" I thought, "Sure, I would feel calm and happy." KNOCK, KNOCK. I immediately looked up from my book. Life has crazy timing sometimes! I forgot a team member would be dropping off some paperwork that morning. My hair was crazy from reclining and reading, and I stood up so fast I was lightheaded. Yet, I didn't panic. I know I am enough, and my current circumstances don't define me.

Happiness does not have to be dependent on you looking amazing, your house being clean, and your kids looking fabulous. You are always enough. Now, still do your best. My home is clean and tidy half the time, and the other half it's messy with projects and things the kids are using. It all depends on what time of day you stop by to knock on our door. One day you might be impressed, and the next day you might think, "I'm glad I don't have to clean that up!" My friend, put forth your best efforts, simplify, and put things in order, yet allow yourself to have imperfect moments.

Reread the quote above. Mandy is basically saying, "Let go of the shoulds, and celebrate your life!" Does that sound familiar at all?

Remember, being happy means to be connected with yourself at your heart-level (body and spirit connected). Your heart energy is turned on, and you feel like "you" again.

UNhappiness

Now let's talk about what happiness is not. When you know what something is not, you better understand what it truly is. Obviously, happiness is not depression and feeling disconnected.

I spent months in what I'll call "light" depression. Some may call this "being in a funk." This is when people don't feel like themselves, but they don't realize that they are feeling slightly depressed.

How do you know when you are experiencing depression? Here are a few possible indicators.

Possible depression/disconnection indicators:

- You don't feel like yourself
- Slumped posture
- Frown most of the time
- Low energy
- Low self-value
- Your thoughts are constantly tearing you down
- Lack motivation to do anything
- Things feel robotic/routine/heartless to you
- Nothing to look forward to in the future
- Look down at the floor a lot
- Head hangs down a lot
- Feel like you have no "heart"
- Your "heart" isn't in what you are doing

Why Happiness?

- Nothing is fun for you
- You yell at others a lot
- Get frustrated really quickly
- Get angry really quickly
- Get very critical of yourself and others
- Try to distract yourself a lot (too much social media and screen time)
- Go from 0 to 100 in negative emotional intensity quickly (calm/quiet to frustration/anger)—this is a great sign that you are below heart-level.
- People ask you at least once a week if you are depressed
- Nothing can make you smile
- Suicidal thoughts [No shame here, it just is. Please don't feel like you're alone in this. Opposing forces nowadays are very strong. Pretty much anyone you meet has had that thought cross their minds, and the deeper the stages of depression, the more intense and believable those thoughts become. Don't trust them. Just say, "Thank you for sharing, but I choose to live."]
- You've thought, "I'll never feel happy again" or "I can't remember the last time I felt happy."
- You think "I hate happy people" or "Happy people are stupid."
- You feel that "Happy is not a possible reality."

Remember, It's OK to feel how you are feeling. Please use caution with the actions you choose to take because of how you are feeling. Feeling angry and upset is separate from criticizing someone or physically hurting them. It's OK and safe to feel; it is not OK to harm yourself or another person.

What is happiness?

Happy is our natural state. UNhappy is just being disconnected from yourself, your HAPPY.

Here are some tips to help you connect and stay connected with your true self:

1. Limit your screen time: keep the first and last hour of your day "screen-free." This gives you time and space to remain connected with yourself. You can use empowerment tools, do your *morning champion training*, read a great book, or review/plan your day. Each night I love to review my wins and celebrations of the day. I recognize and congratulate myself for the good I did that day.
2. "Drops in the bucket." Forget all the "I should have done more …" thoughts. Focus on the good that you *did* do that day. Imagine it like this: every good deed you do adds another drop to your bucket. It all counts.
3. A fabulous way to help lift your spirits is to take the focus off yourself. Forget for a moment how low you're feeling, how nothing is going your way, and all the other blah-blah. Instead, focus on loving and serving others.

Here's a starter list of ideas on how to serve and love others.

Serving others:

- Clean something for someone.
- Pick up trash at a local park.
- Pull weeds in someone else's yard for five minutes or longer.

- Prepare dinner and take it to a friend/young mother's home.
- Babysit someone's children for a few hours.
- Find a way to bring a smile to your family's faces today :)
- Send a simple card with words of affirmation.
- Send flowers or a gift.
- Give meaningful service according to the needs you notice. Observe first, then serve.
- Ask someone, "How can I best support you?" Then follow through with what you say you'll do.
- Simply spend time with them doing something fun.
- Visit the lonely, elderly, or other young mothers in need of support and friendship.
- Search local service projects you could join in your community, pick one, then do it!

Here are more ways to feel happy:

Happiness Tips (arranged by stages)

Stage 1:
- Validate (Build that foundation!)

Stage 2:
- Passively nurture yourself
- Do something to passively put a smile on your face.
  - You can read Chapter 6 of *Being Unhappy Sucks, So STOP IT!* for a great list of ridiculous jokes to help you laugh.

Stage 3:
- Serve someone; take the focus off yourself. Look forward to brightening their day.
- Find or create something to look forward to.

Stage 4:
- Use your voice to connect with others, and ask someone for help and support.
- Connect more by serving someone else.
- Don't say, "I'll be happy when …" or "I'd be happy if only …"
- Don't base happiness on circumstances or anyone or anything else (this just doesn't work).
- Focus on what you DO have (not on what you don't).
- Remember, your happiness is 100% within your own control.

Stage 5:
- Choose to feel happy now.
- Focus on what you CAN control (not what you can't).
- See the good in the world!
- Get out and moving in nature!
- Do your favorite type of physical movement, especially outside! (Run, jog, bike, hike, walk, swim, do yoga, sports, or whatever else you love doing.)

Stage 6:
- Forgive others freely.
- Learn the lessons quickly that life gives you.
- Remember Tony Robbins' wise words, "Everything happens for you, not against you."
- Replace doubtful questions with gratitude.
- Once you've learned the lessons, choose to be present. Choose to be happy now.
- Focus on the NOW. You can only connect with yourself in the present because you only reside in the now. The past or future is where you are not. You are only here right NOW.
- Celebrate! Celebration is the sincerest, highest form of gratitude.

Why Happiness?

Stage 6 includes "Forgive others freely" because forgiving others is healing for your heart. Let's dive into forgiveness for a minute.

Forgiveness matters

"One of the greatest motivations for forgiveness is knowing that it's you who will be the primary beneficiary when you do it. Forgiveness is for you."
~ Barbara J. Hunt

Forgiveness is not about saying that what the other person did was OK (it's not condoning or agreeing with it); it's about releasing that negative emotion from yourself so you can begin to heal. On the flip side, holding grudges literally stops or greatly slows down your healing.

The brilliant Dr. M. T. Morter Jr. added massive value to the world by clearly identifying the necessary steps of forgiveness. The following is based on the Morter forgiveness model.

Four Steps of Forgiveness:

- Recognize your own fault, and forgive yourself
- Forgive the other person completely
- Ask and allow them to forgive you (for holding on to this negative emotion and directing it back at them)
- See the good; learn the lesson

Forgiveness heals your heart.

Forgiveness heals you. It releases the negative and makes room for more positive in your life.

Forgiving more quickly helps you feel more happy.

Forgiveness heals, and to further your happiness journey, you must clear all misconceptions around it. If you misunderstand what happiness truly is, how can you truly find happiness? Are you ready to bust these top five happiness myths? Let's go!

Busting the Happiness Myths

Myth 1:
- "If you seek happiness, you'll never find it."
- "You can't find happiness if you are searching for it."

I call that a lie. Maybe if you don't understand what happiness truly is, you may try to find it in all the wrong places. However, now that you know exactly what happiness is (being connected to yourself at heart-level), you can always find happiness when you are feeling low. Do the action step for each stage you are in, and you will move back up to feeling truly happy again, I promise.

This next one may be controversial, but hear me out.

Myth 2:
- "Money can't buy happiness."

The more correct phrase would be "Money can't buy *joy*." Now what do I mean by that? If looking forward to something reconnects you with yourself at heart-level, and that reconnects you with your natural state of being happy, then if you look forward to purchasing creative supplies, or paying for an amazing experience, then yes, buying something helped you to look forward to something, thus resulting in you feeling happy. Money (indirectly) can buy happiness; It just can't buy joy! Remember this:

Why Happiness?

- Happiness = being connected with your spirit-self at heart-level. Looking forward to something like an experience that may cost money (like a vacation) may bring you happiness and reconnect you with yourself.
- Joy = being connected with God. (Last I checked, you can't buy a connection with God. But good news, He offers that freely to those who "Come unto Him.")

Myth 3:
- "People that laugh and smile are happy."

Now, if you are happy, you will probably smile and laugh more. However, as the brilliant T. Harv Eker teaches:
- "Laughter is laughter, and happy is happy, but they are not the same thing."
- "Fun is fun, and happy is happy, but they are not the same thing."
- "Pleasure is pleasure, and happy is happy, but they are not the same thing."

On the outside you may laugh, have fun, and smile, yet that may be a façade. You may still feel disconnected on the inside.

Have you ever heard that "Wickedness never was happiness"? This is literally true. People may laugh and have fun, yet they cannot be truly happy if they are indulging in self-destructive behavior because that always brings them below heart-level. Happiness is only experienced above heart-level.

So what is "happy" if it's not fun, laughter, or pleasure? I've found it is being connected with your true, higher self at heart-level. When you are above heart-level, your higher self is connected with your more temporal/physical self. Your heart energy is on, so you feel happy. You start to feel like yourself because you are operating from your true self again.

Myth 4:
- "I'll be happy when …"
- "I'd be happy if only …"
- "When …, then I'll be happy."
- "If …, then I'd be happy."

Truth: Happiness is within your control simply because happiness is your natural state. If you're not happy without it, you'll probably not be happy even with it. Happiness focused on outside happenings and circumstances never lasts. If you're not happy now without it happening, if it happened, you'd probably still be unhappy. Choose to connect with yourself and do the actions that will lead to your true happiness.

Myth 5:
- "Do what you should, and then you'll be happy."

Truth: Shoulds never make anyone happy. Quite the opposite. "Should-ing" yourself shames yourself and pushes you deeper into disconnect and depression. Instead, make better decisions by following your heart.

Should-Shame Cycle

More on "Shoulds." If you have a mental "should" list, get rid of it. Remember, shoulds are shaming, and they just push you deeper into disconnect. If you must get that done, rephrase it to say, "I must do this," "I could do this," "I want to do this," or "I get to do this." Or you could completely eliminate, automate, or delegate it so that it is no longer on your personal must-do list.

Should = pushing deeper into disconnect.
Must = determination to get it done because "I want to do it."
Here's another way of saying it. The great Tony Robbins teaches this:

- Depression = life not matching your blueprint/expectations.

If you think your life "should" look a certain way, you will feel somewhat depressed. The "should" says, "It should be this way, but it's never gonna happen." Or at best, "I have to force myself to do it because I don't really want to, but I should." That is very different from thinking, "My life could be like that ..." "Could" feels a lot more like it's a possibility. "Could" feels so much lighter and brighter.

Forcing the should to happen —> depression and disconnection.
Should —> shame —> depression

Allow things to be, and look at positive possibilities. Lighten your load by either deleting your shoulds or changing your shoulds into a "must" or a "could," or "I choose to ..." This will help you stay above heart-level more.

It feels amazing UP here!

My daily focus is to live above heart-level. Everything feels so much better up here. The feelings are much more pleasant.

Here are some examples of what it looks like living below vs. living above heart-level. Remember, below heart-level is where the lies and counterfeits reside. Above heart-level is where truth, authenticity, happiness, and joy live.

Below Heart-Level	Above Heart-Level
It's all about me	It's about others. I show up to love and serve.
Depressed/UNhappy	Feeling happy
Reactive	Proactive and lovingly responsive
Annoyed	Calm, and understanding of others
Should	Can, Must, Will
Critical	Nonjudgmental
Hateful	Loving and supportive
Hurting so bad that you hurt others too	So full of self-love that your abundance pours love into others as well
Feeling "not enough"	Confident
Everything happens to me	Everything happens for me
Pessimistic or "realistic"	Optimistic
Problem-focused	Solutions-focused
Manipulative (creating win-lose or lose-lose situations)	Persuasive (creating win-win situations)
Take energy	Create energy
"I'll never feel happy again."	"I love feeling so happy!"
Scarcity mentality: "There's not enough. There's nothing good for me."	Abundance mentality: "There's more than enough resources and happiness for everyone."
Feelings are unpleasant (anger, boredom, criticism, frustration)	Feelings are pleasant (happy, excited, calm, loving)
Nobody cares	I care about me and others

Here's a feelings/emotions list showing the difference between what it feels like to live below or above heart-level. This chart was inspired by a children's feelings chart from Generationmindful.com.

Feelings chart: Above and Below Heart-Level:

Below heart-level: Higher energetic charge	Above heart-level feelings: Higher energy
Angry	Happy
Inflexible, one way to do it. Do it my way.	Flexible
Confused, uncertain	Brave, determined
Anxious, worried, fearful (anticipating discomfort/pain)	Excited (anticipating pleasure)
Frustrated	Find humor in things not turning out as expected, feeling silly and fun
Mad	Joyful
Jealous	Celebrating others' successes Proud of your own accomplishments
Scared	Pleasantly surprised

Below heart-level: lower energy	Above heart-level: lower/calm energy
Sad	Calm
Critical	Reflective
Bored	Caring
Disappointed	Kind and Understanding
Embarrassed	Grateful, and learn from mistakes
Lonely	Loving
Tired	Peaceful, Fulfilled
Worried	Relaxed

Do you see how much more pleasant it is to live above heart-level? Everything feels better when you are above heart-level. The main difference between the left column and the right is, "Are you living above heart-level?" If not, it doesn't feel so good. If so, life feels wonderful!

Tiny action

- Write down, "My daily goal is to be above heart-level."

- Pro tip: If currently your daily set point is being happy at heart-level, then write down, "My daily goal is is to be joyful and fully connected.

    Now give yourself a high five and say, "I am amazing!"

STUMBLING BLOCKS

"Quiet the mind, and the soul will speak."
~ Ma Jaya Sati Bhagavati

"I don't get it. I do everything I can to lift myself UP, and then I wake up the next day feeling low again." Seriously, this just happened. I worked each day to lift myself UP, and then I'd have a weird dream or something, and I'd wake up below heart-level again. I didn't get it. Why? No matter how hard I tried, I still ended up feeling low. The lower I got, the less motivation I had to try to feel better. And then I realized that I was tripping over my own stumbling block.

Three days earlier, I felt totally excited and inspired. My heart said yes to taking a class that would help bring me joy and fulfillment and further spread my message. I'd always wanted to learn how to use these elements of creation and design. What was stopping me? I knew it was right and had no reason not to, yet I didn't take immediate action. My soul didn't let me get away with that procrastination any longer, and I began to feel it. I kept dropping below heart-level and feeling a little off. My soul reminded me that I'd promised myself I would do something, and I would probably keep feeling low like this until I actually took action on this inspiration! As soon as I figured that out, I immediately purchased the class, and now I'm loving it! As soon as I took action on my inspiration, that "funk" totally dissipated, and I moved back up above heart-level. It feels so much better UP here!

As you seek to stay above heart-level, you may come across many of these stumbling blocks. When you recognize them, you can take proper action to step over them and keep moving forward.

Stumbling block #1: Inaction

Inspiration without application/expression can lead to depression.

This was exactly what I just experienced. I was inspired, my heart said "YES!" and I made a decision to do it, but then I hesitated. Three days later, I began to slip lower and lower, until I realized what had happened. I finally chose to follow my heart.

Think of it this way: Have you ever had an idea to do something and gotten excited about it? Then maybe a thought came like, "You can't do that." Maybe you felt like, "I could never do that. I'm too _____. I don't have enough _____. People will think _____." Those shaming, stopping thoughts don't feel so good, do they? Your spirit sinks, and you may say, "Forget it. It's just not meant to be." You end up feeling worse than before, am I right? Our spirits rise at the thought of creation, progress, and possibilities, but our spirits sink at the thought of being unable to act and not following through with the inspiration.

Our hearts know what is good for us and will lead us toward progression and true happiness. Our hearts will always lead us toward good. You can know it's inspiration if it guides you forward. If it leads you to do good, it is good.

On the other hand, doubt and fear will seek to pull you backward, and you will begin to fall below heart-level.

Inspiration (-) application —> depression

Stumbling Blocks

Why is this? *Decisions without action turn into shoulds.*

Should —> shame —> depression

Maybe an idea comes and you say, "I'll do it!" When hesitation comes in, you think, "Maybe I'll do it," then, "I don't know, maybe not," until lastly, "Forget it." Can you just feel your heart sink lower with each successive thought in that line? Bottom line, when you decide to do something, do it!

To increase your happiness and success, shorten the line between decisions and action:

Decision-----------------------(room for doubt)-----------------------Action

Decision—Action

(no room for doubt, just action and progression)

When you make a decision, follow the seven-day rule. My mentoring clients know that once you decide to do something, you must take action toward it within the next one to seven days. When you make a decision, the first step is to write it down and schedule when you will be doing that first step toward completing that action. After seven days, the decision becomes a "should" and a mental weight because your brain has to keep reminding you that you chose to do it (until you actually do it)!

For example, when you declutter and choose to give away your excess stuff, you must actually give it away within those first seven days. If you have an ever-growing donation pile of stuff in your garage, it then starts to be a "should" and a mental weight until you actually follow through with your decision to give it away. Remember, must-do without action —> should (then shame, then depression). Stop the should-shame cycle by taking action! Either remove that from your list (by delegation or deletion), or turn it into a decided action and do it!

Action energy is greatest at the beginning of a decision. The sooner you take action, the greater the energy you create to follow through with that action. Use that "starter energy" to your advantage by taking quick action whenever you make a decision to act. Decide first, then act quickly on that decision. Take that first step in the right direction to create momentum.

Pro tip: Keep the first step easy and doable to get started. Make the first step the easiest!! If it's ridiculously easy to get started, then you're more likely to actually do it!

- Decisions without action degenerate into shoulds.
- Decisions with action generate creation energy!

Stumbling block #2: Not keeping commitments

Keep UP above heart-level by keeping all your commitments. Only commit to and say YES to what you truly intend to do. Learn to say no to "shoulds" and say yes to your YESs.

You can practice keeping your commitments by keeping your time commitments. I used to be a chronic "late arrival." There was always one more thing I could try to get done before I had to leave, or I would only give myself the exact number of minutes it would take to drive there in the best traffic. Have you ever done this? No margin and no room for error. Well, that generally leads to being late, even just 1–2 minutes, but that's still late. Have you ever hoped the meeting would start late just so you'd feel like you didn't miss anything? That becomes pretty stressful, wouldn't you agree? I hope I'm not the only one who's ever done that.

One day, I opened my email to find a bonus training I'd earned. Wow, this forever changed my life! I learned that whenever you make a commitment and keep it, your brain rewards you with a burst of energy. I tried it out. I began to keep my time commitments to the minute, and I felt a major difference in my energy levels.

Stumbling Blocks

Let's practice. If you say to yourself you'll wake up at 7:00 a.m., then actually do it. If you tell someone you'll meet them at 3:00, then you plan to arrive early so that no matter what the outside circumstances (like traffic), you always have a margin of extra time. Arrive early, stay happy, and receive that burst of energy.

Do this with something tiny. For example, say, "At 11:30 a.m. I will begin to prepare lunch." Make sure you are in the kitchen beginning preparations by 11:29 a.m., and recognize and celebrate yourself for your accomplishment! You kept your commitment!

If you want more happiness and energy, keep your commitments.

If you need to renegotiate the time, always do it before the first time has passed. If you say, "I will start getting ready for bed at 10 p.m.," and you realize you will be a little later, renegotiate before the original time has come and say, "I will get up to go to bed by 10:15 p.m." When you keep your new commitment to yourself, you will still get the "burst of energy" reward.

If you need to renegotiate with someone else, always ask permission far in advance before the set time has come. Ask, "I know we agreed upon __ o'clock, but would it be OK if we changed it to __ o'clock?" If they don't agree with the change, then still keep the original agreement. Respect yourself and others enough to keep your commitments. Remember, only commit to what you actually can and will do! Only say yes when you mean it.

Pro mommy tip: Whenever I plan to leave the house with all my kids, I give myself three different times. At ____ we begin to get ready. At ____ we are getting into the car. By ___ we are driving away. For example, my son's karate starts at 4 p.m., so we begin to get ready at 3:20, we start getting everyone buckled into the car at 3:30, and we need to be driving away by 3:40 (10–15 minutes to drive there, plus a 5-minute buffer). I give myself plenty of margin because either someone can't find shoes, or the baby has a poopy diaper explosion, or something happens to cause delays. I prepare for delays and then get on my way. (I'm not perfect, but I can often handle setbacks and still get to places on time.) The more kids I have, the more time I give myself for us to all be ready to go. More kids = more possibilities of unexpected delays, so I give us more getting-ready time.

Another way to keep your commitments is to make them small enough to easily achieve. Make a tiny commitment, then keep it! I love the book *Mini Habits* by Stephen Guise because it highlights the power of tiny commitments. Keeping it simple and doable can build huge momentum and progress. Can I let you in on a secret? I wrote this entire book in just three months because of a tiny commitment. When I started, my goal each day was to write for at least one minute. Since that was so easy, I kept that commitment every day. Some days I only wrote 50 words. Other days, I started writing and didn't look up until three-plus hours later. One day I worked on this for more than eight hours straight! My tiny commitment kept the momentum going on those days when I didn't feel I had time to write, but I wrote for that one minute anyway, and it helped me keep this going until completion. Try making small commitments for yourself and then keeping them! It really works.

No matter how tiny, each step in the right direction is worth it.

Each time you keep a commitment to yourself, you feel a little happier and more confident. Confidence comes from knowing that what you say is what you do. Your word is your bond. Your words are always true. You do what you say no matter what. Now that is power. If you desire to increase your confidence, only say yes to things you will do, then ALWAYS do it. The more you trust yourself, the more confident you will be. The more you keep your commitments, the happier you will become.

Stumbling block #3: Blocking inspiration

I like to think there's a great inspiration department up in the sky that loves giving us ideas. Ideas and inspirations flow down to us all the time. "But Heather, how can that be? I never have inspiration or any great ideas." Maybe you've been blocking the inspiration. Imagine ideas falling like raindrops, but you hold up an umbrella and all the raindrop inspirations then fall onto your neighbor. I like to call this the Umbrella Effect. If you block it out, of course you're not receiving it. What happens when we close ourselves off to receiving? It goes to someone else. If you want to receive more, put your umbrella down and work through these inspiration blockers.

Inspiration blockers

1. **Not having a Higher Power.**
   If you're relying on just yourself, how are you supposed to make progress? You only know what you know, and you don't know everything you don't know. Reconnect to the Source of all light, love, knowledge, and wisdom, and be willing to receive more.

2. **Not writing it down.**
   Do you ever get an amazing idea and say, "I'll write it down later"? What happens? Most likely you'll forget it before you get around to actually writing it down. Start the habit now of writing down everything immediately! I have a five-second rule for myself. I write down all ideas and inspirations within five seconds of receiving it. (My kids know I keep a pen in my hair so I can grab it and write things down quickly.) Keep a pen and

paper (or your phone) nearby, so you can always write down ideas quickly. Usually when I write one idea down, many more ideas come. Often the first idea is a test to see if I value the idea. When I accept that idea by writing it down, many times I'm given a whole treasure chest of brilliant ideas right after that. We'll never know what treasures of inspirations we could be receiving until we simply accept and act upon the smaller "test" ideas.

3. Not doing it.
If you feel like you don't get a lot of inspiration, chances are you've received ideas in the past but never took action on them. If you don't take action on the inspiration, you're not being a good steward over it. If this happens enough times, ideas stop getting through to you. Inaction clogs your system. You'll probably be given more ideas and inspirations again when you begin to take immediate action on what you feel inspired to do. The first action with an idea is to write it down! Remember, inspiration will always guide you forward. It will feel peaceful, good, and positive in your heart. If it leads you to do good, it is good.

4. Your mind is too full.
If your mind is too full, nothing else can fit in! Empty your mind, and write things down to get them out of your head. Give yourself quiet, empty space in your day. Have you noticed that the best ideas tend to come to you in the shower or while you're falling asleep? The inspirations can finally get through to you when your mind has quieted down enough for you to listen. If you intentionally give yourself more quiet space in your day, more inspirations can get through to you. Try going for a quiet walk to help clear your mind and refresh your soul.

Receiving Inspiration

Use the AWDRR principle to open up and receive inspiration.

Ask: Each morning, look up and ask, "What is my action step today?" Listen for the answer, because these daily, purposeful action steps will help you progress in your goals. (If you don't have goals, maybe your action step for today is to write down and commit to two or three goals!)

Write: Write down your action step!

Do: Do your action step each day.

Report: Each night, report that you fulfilled your action step. Celebrate your accomplishment!

Receive the reward: Sometimes the reward comes as a spark of happiness in your heart. You may receive an unexpected gift, or your income might increase. Sometimes the reward comes as a new download of inspiration, or you may receive your next inspired action step. Whatever the reward, receive it with a grateful heart and continue progressing and growing!

Ask. Write. Do. Report. Receive the reward.

Stumbling block #4: Procrastination

When I have too much on my mind, it begins to weigh me down. Sometimes it's so overwhelming that I start to avoid the most important things. I tend to clean my house the most when I am avoiding doing something I know I need to do. Have you ever done that? Are you very productive on the little things because you're avoiding the bigger things? Avoidance is a strong motivator. However, it doesn't always motivate us to do the most important things. When I start avoiding important things or my mind is feeling weighed down, I write out a procrastination list.

Try this now: Get a piece of paper and completely empty your mind of everything you have to do. Write down everything you've been putting off. Once you've got it all written out, start completing some of the tasks and crossing them off your list. This will free up a lot of your mental energy (because your brain no longer has to hold space for that task and send you frequent reminders). If possible, either delegate or totally eliminate some of the items. If it's not helping you progress and move forward or making your life better in some way, delete it if you can. This is like decluttering your brain and mental to-do list. Get rid of the nonessentials and start making progress on the things of value. Doesn't it feel great to get a lot of this done and checked off your list? You've got this!

Stumbling block #5: The five FIMEJ filters

I prefer filtered water because it always tastes much better. Filters hold back the parts that don't belong so that the water is clearer and fresher. Life does the same with us. Five main filters are put in place to test us and see how committed we are to getting our desired results. Are we willing to do what it takes to get through these filters? When you get through the filters, life is clearer and more refreshing on the other side.

Let's briefly introduce these filters and see how to get through each one.

Fear

Fear is the anticipation of discomfort/pain.

Use these three main actions to overcome fear:

1. Since fear comes when you anticipate discomfort, turn it around to anticipate pleasure instead. Ask yourself, "How can I make this process more enjoyable?" Transform the anticipation of discomfort into expecting pleasure. Find ways to enjoy the process more.
2. Face it head-on to lessen its intensity. Action dispels fear.
3. Increase your faith. Faith and fear cannot coexist in the same space at the same time. Fear is living below heart-level, and faith is better experienced when living above heart-level. Focus on living above heart-level to experience more hope, happiness, joy, faith, light, love, and progress.

Inconvenience

If something felt right in your heart and you knew it would totally transform your life, would you do whatever it takes to make it happen? Inconvenience stops the uncommitted, the "I'll try if I can" or the "maybe someday ..." To get through this filter, decide what results you desire, be 100% committed, and embody the attitude of "If it's right, I do it No Matter What."

Money

Money is potential love and service. Money is a way to share value and service to people all over this world. Without money and trade, we'd be on our own to grow food and support ourselves. Money is a neutral, helpful tool. Love other people enough to give and receive money.

Money is a beautiful symbol of our human connection and collaboration.

The money filter sounds a lot like, "I could never do that," "I can't afford that," or, "People with money are (judgmental comment)." Instead, bless that which you desire. Bless and send light and love to those who have more, and you may just start receiving more too. Earth is abundantly wealthy, and there are more than enough resources for everyone. Scarcity thinking is living below heart-level, but viewing the world abundantly is living above heart-level. Which one feels better to you?

If you value the option in front of you enough, then spend money on it. Invest in growing yourself, your mind, abilities, enjoyment, and celebration. When options arise, say "Yes!" to the yes's and "no thank you" to the no's. If it's something you desire, yet it costs more than you currently have, ask yourself, "How can I afford that?" or "How could I create the resources to receive that?" When you decide no, simply say, "I choose not to right now," or "No thank you."

Embarrassment

The sting of embarrassment doesn't feel good. Many people will do almost anything to avoid potential embarrassment. Can I share a secret? The more often you do uncomfortable things, the less intense the fear of embarrassment gets. Public speaking is most people's number-one fear, yet if you do it often enough, you realize that when you share your message from your heart, there is nothing to fear. When you speak from your heart with the intention to serve, you can have fun with it, learn to laugh at your mistakes, and play along with the audience. The more you do something, the more comfortable you get with the uncomfortable. Dr. Roland Phillips taught me, "It's only difficult until it's not." Keep taking your action steps. It's only going to be uncomfortable until it's not.

Judgment

Fearing judgment has been my biggest stopper in the past. I'm a recovering people-pleaser because I don't like to upset people. Hiding because of fear of judgment doesn't really work with my desire to spread my message to the world. Chances are at least some people will not like me. Nobody on earth has 100% popularity among all people. Opinions and preferences differ, and not everyone will like you or what you do. The only way to never find people who dislike you is to avoid all people, but that doesn't work out very well either.

The sooner you get over the fear of judgment, the sooner you can be your truly authentic self, loving your life and living your purpose. The best way I have found to do this is to love people more. Send your message, products, and services with love and be unattached to outcomes. Do your best work and send it with love. I am writing this book from my heart, and I know some people might not like it. They might criticize, yet I'm writing this anyway, knowing that if this helps even one young mother lift herself UP above heart-level, feel connected and happy again, then this is all worth it just for her. Even though some people may not like you, love people enough to love and serve them anyway. Honor yourself, love others, and celebrate together.

Stumbling block #6: Dropping below heart-level

Stay UP!

"How are you feeling, honey?" I replied, "Terrible." Eric said, "I feel like something amazing is coming, let's stay UP and see what the reward is." My husband left for the clinic, and I still sat on the couch miserable. Twenty minutes later, I heard a knock on the door. I almost wanted to just ignore it and wish they'd go away, but instead I opened the door. A delivery guy handed me a bag of food with my name on it. I shut the door, looked at the yummy food (my favorite!), and I nearly cried. My sweet husband had ordered me breakfast to give me a lift and put a little smile on my face. I felt a little lighter and decided I did want to feel better that day. I remembered to look forward to good things coming my way. I lifted myself back up above heart-level. The best part is that later that day my husband received an unexpected $13,000 check; that's quite a reward for staying UP! And no joke, a package arrived on my doorstep because I'd won a prize! We stayed up above heart-level, and the rewards came.

The rewards usually come after a strong test. Isn't it true that the darkest of the night always comes before the sun rises? When doubt comes in, you know your reward is so close! This pattern is so universal, it's funny to watch! Many times I've been in line for something, and someone ahead of me has been waiting a long time. Literally just one to three minutes before it's their turn, they give up and move over to a different line. As soon as they do, this line moves forward and it would have been their turn.

The doubt ALWAYS comes right before the reward just to test us. Watch this and see if it isn't true. Pay attention to when you start feeling that doubt, and watch the time to see how many minutes pass until it's your turn. On the bigger things, it might be days or weeks before the reward comes when the doubt begins, but just start paying attention. When chaos hits and you are tempted to doubt, stay UP! Your reward is so close!!

We receive rewards when we remain UP above heart-level. Think of it like this: We walk along in life, and a reward is placed in our path. Then tests and trials come. If we drop below heart-level, we drop below the line where the reward is waiting, we keep walking forward, and we've passed the reward. When we finally get back up above heart-level, we've already missed the reward. Have you ever felt like, "I thought something amazing was coming my way, but it never came"? If you stay above heart-level, you receive more of life's wonderful rewards.

We call this the Stay UP! principle. Chaos always happens right before a higher level of order. When the chaos hits, do your best to look forward to the reward that's so close to you, and stay UP! Remember, looking forward to something lifts you back up above heart-level, so look forward to your reward! If everything suddenly goes to chaos in your home (car breaks down, fridge starts leaking, toilet gets clogged, and everyone's unhappy), just stay UP. Your reward is so close. In that moment, take a few deep breaths and tell yourself, "I can handle this. Things always get better. I've got this." Remind your family to stay up, and tell them a reward is probably on its way. You don't know what it is, but it's gonna be good. Watch miracles happen in your life when you choose to stay up above heart-level especially when the chaos hits.

> *"You miss the miracles when your energy is low."*
> ~ Kisma Orbovich

On the flip side, you experience miracles when you live from your heart.

Raise your energy, and stay above heart-level. When your heart energy is on, amazing things happen. When you are living from love and abundance, the world around you changes. If you don't believe me, try to prove me wrong. Live above heart-level for the next 30 days straight, and tell me if things around you don't change. They will, because when you live from your heart, you naturally desire to progress and improve your life. You treat others more kindly and with more compassion, and life feels so amazing. I know you've got this!

Remember, the rewards always come. Get through the filters, stay UP, and receive the reward.

The UNdepressed Heart

Stumbling block #7: Focus on problems

"Everyone who found the solution, raise your hand." I raised my hand and looked around; out of 200+ people, only one other person (the smartest guy in the room) had his hand raised. How had I figured out the puzzle? I assure you, I wasn't smarter than any of the others in that training. Many had vast amounts more knowledge than me, so what did I do differently? The trainer put up a word puzzle. We were asked to figure out the pattern of similarity between these seemingly unrelated words: BANANA, ROLLO, KIWI. Most people gave up after a few minutes of frustrating results.

I decided to play with it. I looked for possibilities. Facetiously I thought, "All the words are black. They are all in English. They all have vowels. They all have consonants. They are all foods. They are written in all caps." The more similarities I acknowledged when my brain gave me an idea, the more possibilities my brain produced. After finding multiple ridiculous similarities, a few minutes passed, and I finally found it! I finally saw the connection between all the words! Since I had kept my mind open to possibilities, I found the answer. (Send me a message when you see the answer too!)

The thing with the brain is when you say, "I don't know," it stops working and gives up trying. But if you say, "What are the possibilities here?" your brain will go looking for the answer. It will give you everything it finds, even ridiculous answers. The key is to acknowledge every idea by writing it down. When you reward your brain for every idea it gives you and you say, "That's a possibility," your brain continues to give you more possibilities.

I do this with my kids all the time. When they're feeling low and wanting to do something fun, we create a "possibilities list." We write down all the fun things they can think of (whether plausible for that

Stumbling Blocks

day or not, I still write them all down). When we've got all our ideas out, we choose the idea that is a win for both me and the kids. For example, going to Disneyland sounds amazing and fun, but it's not an option for today. However, making a treat and going to the splash park is both fun for them and doable for me. It's a win-win.

When life gets difficult, it's easy to only see all the problems in front of you. The problem is that what you focus on expands. If you see only problems, that's all you're going to see. If you're focused only on problems, your vision is blocked and you miss seeing the possible solutions. The Law of Polarity states that everything has an opposite. If the opposite of your problems are possibilities, then you have hope to change things in your life. For every problem, there is a solution. Be open to seeing more solutions.

Try this now: Write down a problem in your life you'd like to create a solution for. Write out 100 possible solutions for it. It's very important to write down all the ideas as they come. Don't dismiss any, or you'll begin to block off the rest of the ideas. Write them ALL down (you'll filter them out later). Keep going until you feel your brain has emptied all possible solutions. Look upward and ask, "Are there any more?" If so, write more. When completed, look at your list and cross off any implausible ideas. Only keep legal, moral, ethical, and plausible ideas. Look at your list: Are there possible win-win solutions to help with the problem? If so, congratulations! You listed all possibilities, and your brain rewarded you with the best solution.

Whenever you find yourself getting stuck, try creating a possibilities list and see what magical solutions you come up with. You may just surprise yourself!

- Problems expand below heart-level
- Solutions exist above heart-level

Get yourself up above heart-level and seek possible solutions. Say these affirmations out loud to yourself right now:
- I am a solutions maker!
- I seek and create solutions.
- I seek creative, win-win solutions.
- I always find a solution where everybody wins.
- I am a solutions creator.

Now give yourself a high five and say, "Yes, I am!"

Focus on solutions. Solutions are so much easier to find when you are above heart-level. When you are connected to yourself and the Source of all inspiration, solutions come more easily to your mind. Once you see a possible solution, act on it. Sometimes you may even find multiple solutions, and then you get to experiment and see which one works best. Which one creates a win-win situation for you and others?

When a disagreement arises, it's best to find "third-party solutions." Brainstorm together on all possibilities to figure out a third-party solution. This solution is usually something neither party had even thought of before. Mastermind with others, and see what possibilities you can come up with. Remember, in brainstorming sessions, *all ideas are valid*. Write all the ideas down! You can sort them all out later, but write everything down as it comes.

One last thing. When you are above heart-level, you grow yourself bigger than your problems. Many lesser problems dissipate when you are living true to yourself. Everything you used to get annoyed or frustrated at no longer bothers you. You either find and implement creative win-win solutions or the situations may seem to resolve themselves. Either way, living life up above heart-level is the goal, because it feels so much better UP here!

Stumbling block #8: Not identifying with your true self

We English speakers have a real disadvantage. We confuse our states of being with our identity all too easily because both are prefaced with the statement "I am." Like, "I am cold," instead of, "I am feeling cold." Or, "I am sad," instead of, "I am feeling sad. "I am depressed," instead of, "I am experiencing depression." Let's make this very clear: you are not your problems. You are not your roles. You are not your past mistakes. You are not what you do. You are a being of light. You are you. You are precious. Your value and worth are intrinsically priceless simply because you are you.

In order to feel happy and connected with yourself, only identify with your true being. Don't fall into the trap of identifying with depression. Never say, "I am depressed." Instead say, "I am experiencing depression," or, "I am feeling_____."

Another good point: your true identity is based on *being*, not *doing*. You consist of positive attributes, not roles. If you ever feel "lost" in your role as a mother or anything else, you are probably identifying too much with your role and not with who you are. Brooke Snow, author of *Living in Your True Identity*, teaches that you can differentiate your roles from your identity by saying, "I am a_____." Whatever follows the "a" is your role. If you want to identify more of the characteristics and attributes which make up your true identity, simply say, "I am_____." I am powerful. I am amazing. I am loving. I am glorious. I am love.

What you identify with, you act accordingly. Choose your *perception* of your identity wisely. Your true identity never changes, but you can change your perception of your identity to more closely match your *true* identity. The more clearly you can see yourself as the goddess, the truly amazing woman you are, the more connected, happy, and joyful you will become.

Your difficulties do not define you. Your past does not define you. You have a choice, right now, to choose to become your best, love your life, and live above heart-level and UP into full connection and joy.

Stumbling block #9: Putting yourself last

If you forget to care for yourself, you're on the road to burnout. Not giving yourself nurture, rest, and rejuvenation is a major error. You must value the time it takes to truly care for yourself. Time spent giving yourself nurture is never wasted. Time spent doing something that makes you smile helps lift you up. You are most loving and productive when you're above heart-level, so give yourself plenty of nurturing to help you stay UP! Whenever you feel like you need it, do everything you can to help yourself feel nurtured and loved. Maybe think of yourself like a little child needing comfort and love. Give yourself as much positive, comforting love as you can.

You best love and serve others when your own tank is full. If you're running on empty, you're not running anymore. If you put yourself last, or don't value your own self-care and nurturing, you're going to burn out. Burnout happens when there's no more fuel left.

It's not a failure if you drop below heart-level. It's not a failure to drop down to Stage 1. It's not a failure if you feel anxious, fearful, or worried. It just means you are human. Difficult things happen to everyone, and we all feel really crappy sometimes. Just be aware of what stage you are in and what emotions you are experiencing. If necessary, healthfully release those emotions (cry, journal, or go somewhere alone and talk/yell it out). When the emotional storm passes, focus on lifting yourself up just a little to that next stage. You will probably stumble and fall at some point, but you know how to lift yourself back up faster than before. Self-nurturing is a very important step to getting back up.

Take time each day to care for and nurture yourself. This can be simple or it can be grand. Do what you can each day to show yourself you love and care. You are worthy of loving care.

Give yourself plenty of nurture. That way when you take mental/emotional hits, you have a large store of nurturing and the hits won't hurt as much. You'll be able to bounce back UP above heart-level much quicker. If you constantly feel depleted, it's really difficult to get back up. Heart-level living may seem unattainable when you're not being cared for. You must take excellent care of yourself! You are totally worth it!

Practice self-care and nurturing every day. This could look as simple as taking a shower and brushing your hair. This could be taking five minutes to plan your day. This could be giving yourself positive self-talk. You could smile lovingly at yourself in the mirror. Be creative and find ways to love and care for yourself more.

Also, schedule some "white space" into every day. This could include anything that calms your mind:
- Deep breathing
- Walks in nature
- Warm bath to calm your thoughts
- Quiet reading
- Hugs and snuggles with those you love

Find what works and feels good to you. You'll know because your heart will feel expansive, loving, and your core being will feel loved and nurtured. Care for yourself. Love yourself. Fill yourself with loving nurturing.

Stumbling block #10: Listening to the wrong advice

Who do you listen to? Who you listen to, you become like. Notice the people you spend time with, both in person and virtually. What messages are they sending you? Are they supporting you or weakening you? Does it feel good when you're around them or do you feel a bit uneasy?

We adopt attitudes and viewpoints, actions and feelings from people even when we don't realize it. We become more like the people we spend time with. Choose to be around people who build you up and make you feel amazing. True friends help bring out the best in us.

Don't listen to people who have results opposite to what you desire. If you are seeking to release weight, look to someone who has successfully done that and is healthy and happy. If you wish to be a loving, calm mother, don't take parenting advice from someone who yells all the time. If you want to eat healthy, don't ask the person at the fast-food counter what foods you should eat. Don't ask broke friends for investment tips or money advice (even though they will freely give you their opinions)! Don't listen to unhappy people tell you how to truly be happy. Does this make sense?

All my mentors agree and tell people this: don't listen to the news. It's sensationalized and is often very negative. It's a for-profit business: negative news sells more, so that's what they produce. It's how it is, but I don't have to listen to it. The world truly is a grand, amazing place, so seek sources that tell you more of the grandeur and goodness in the world. Focus on the positive to create more love and goodness in this world.

Seek out people who have the results and characteristics you desire, and listen to them. Follow their example, and follow their advice. Only listen to people who have the results you desire to create and the characteristics you wish to develop. Listen to people who help you become better.

Listen to people who are ahead of you. Listen to people you'd love to trade places with. Listen to the people who've already found

Stumbling Blocks

solutions to your problems. The world is so interconnected now, it's amazing! We can learn from people who have found positive, creative solutions to so many of life's challenges. Listen to people who lift, love, create, and bring you greater happiness, love, and fulfillment.

Whew! That's a lot. Did you get all that? Recognize these ten stumbling blocks for what they are, and practice stepping over them. Now take a moment and stretch your arms up and over your head. Take a deep breath in, and let it all out. You're awesome!

Tiny action

- Empty your mind: Write out your procrastination list.

- Remember to stay UP!

Bonus points!

- Clear your mind and heart, then write down all inspirations that come to you!

- Choose one inspiration this week and take action on it.

    Give yourself a high five and say, "I am amazing!"

The UNdepressed Heart

GIVING REAL SUPPORT

How to best support someone who is experiencing depression

"Darkness cannot drive out darkness; only light can do that. Hate cannot drive out hate; only love can do that."
~ Martin Luther King Jr.

May I add to Dr. King's powerful words:
"Shame cannot drive out depression; only validation and unconditional love can do that."

"I just feel so angry." I looked at her with compassion and said, "Then feel angry." If I'd had more time with her, I would have had her jump up, yell, scream, and express all her anger. She looked at me with confusion at first, sizing me up to see if I really meant it. I said quietly again, "Be angry. It's OK." With a tear in her eye, she realized my sincerity. I believe I was the first person ever to give her permission to feel how she was feeling.

Have you ever had someone tell you, "You shouldn't feel that way"? (In case you're wondering, that's exactly what NOT to say to someone, especially if they are experiencing depression.)

Her entire life she grew up feeling so angry at what she was experiencing. She felt so disconnected and unloved, but all she ever heard from people trying to help was, "You shouldn't feel angry. You should be grateful for all your parents did for you. Just get over it already."

Does that ever help? No. Does that automatically make the person say, "Yeah, I shouldn't feel angry, so I'm done"? No! It pushes them deeper into shame and depression. Why? The key word here is "should."

To "should" someone is to shame someone, and shame pushes us deeper into depression. How does this work? A "should" denotes that the person has no control over the action. For example, "I should have said something different." That shows that "should" was in the past, but we can't rewrite the past—it just is.

If you say, "I should go talk to my boss and …" That still denotes lack of ability to take action, or at the very least, a begrudgingly difficult chore of a task. If the should is in the future, "I should go …," then you are still taking yourself out of the present. As we know:

Being present = being connected to your true self = Happy.

Our natural state is Happy. When you are connected to yourself, you are happy because happy is your natural, original state of being.

Should = Shame

Could = Possibilities

Remember, shame is the problem, never the solution.

Let me repeat, shame creates depression, and it is NEVER the solution!!!

For you visual learners, here are shame and guilt on the Six Stages Heart-Level scale:

Guilt alerts us that we did something wrong - it inspires us to change and become better.

Guilt

Shame

Shame is the counterfeit - it pulls us down and shames us into hiding.

Shame and guilt actually manifest themselves as real physical pain in the body. It's fascinating, because guilt-caused physical pain is always above heart-level, and shame-caused pain manifests itself on the body below the heart-level.

Shame vs. Guilt

Shame = Hiding. Shame causes you to hide yourself and your feelings. Shame pushes you deeper into depression.

Guilt = Godly emotion. Guilt helps you realize you've done something wrong and need to make it right again.

These are two totally different things. Guilt is a genuine feeling to help you progress and move forward. Shame is the counterfeit trying to get you to stop progressing. Shame pushes you to hide and disconnect from yourself and all others. *Guilt will never put you below heart-level.* Shame is the counterfeit, and it is craftily designed by opposing forces to pull you below heart-level.

Are you getting this? This is extremely important to understand:
- Guilt inspires change.
- Shame depresses into hiding.

This is a subject that needs to be better understood by all. We can better support our loved ones when we stop shaming. We must validate and truly listen to understand what they are actually experiencing. No more "should-ing" other people! Just cut that word out of your vocabulary! Replace it with "could." Say instead, "I could do that." Whenever you make a suggestion say, "If you'd like, you could …" That gives them more of an option to say yes or no. A "could" feels good, but the "should" makes it feel like you're not good enough if you don't do what you "should." Let people know they have a choice by using "could" because the "could" makes it feel like either option is totally OK to choose.

Let me ask you this: How do you feel when I say this?
- "You really should get up and clean your house for the next hour."

Now I'll rephrase it, and see if it doesn't cause you to feel a little different:
- "You know, you could go clean your house for an hour if you wanted to."

Which feels better to you, the "should" or the "could"? Which one feels like you are obligated, and which one feels more like you have options because whichever you choose is OK?

Remember, shoulds shame because they denote that you are "less than" if you don't. They either communicate that you are incapable of doing that "should" because it's already passed ("I should have done that!"), or you are unwilling/you don't want to ("I should call my friend … but …").

Shoulds shame, and shame depresses. If you wish to feel better, eliminate all "shoulds" from your life. In fact, tear up and throw away your "to-should-myself" list. Instead of telling yourself and others what they "should" do, offer options by saying, "If you wanted to, you could …"

"Should" language leads to stuck living. Possibility thinking and creativity leads to living more freely.

When lifting yourself and others up out of shame and shoulds, remember there is a way UP! Self-love and acceptance lift you higher.

Try this: Continuously tap your heart and say this out loud, starting with your name:

- "[Name], I deeply and completely love and accept you." (Repeat three times)
- "Even though I _____ (insert something you feel shame for), I deeply and completely love and accept you, [Name]." (Repeat three times)
- "Why do I deeply and completely love and accept myself?" (Repeat three times)
- "I am Love. I am loving. I am loved. I am Love." (Repeat three times)

Receive this self-love and acceptance by holding your hand over your heart for a moment. Now take a deep breath in, and blow it out through your mouth. You've got this, girl!

There is hope! You will need to know which stage you are at, so you know what you can do to lift yourself just a little bit higher. The deeper you are, the darker, heavier, and more hopeless it feels. But know this, there is always hope, even if it's just to move up one small step. Small progress is still progress. Slow progress is still progress. All progress is worth it.

When talking with someone else, try to find out which stage they are at. You can now meet them exactly where they are and help them at the level where they need it most.

When you are uncertain of how to help someone, always listen unconditionally with an open heart and validate!

I'll repeat: When in doubt, VALIDATE!

How to best validate others:
- Say something like, "Wow, you must be feeling …"
- "That must be really difficult."
- "That must feel really (terrible, crappy, terrifying, hurtful, sad, lonely, etc.)"
- Be sincere in all this. If you heartlessly try to validate (or worse, sarcastically say it—sarcasm tears down people faster than anything else), that can put them deeper into shame and depression. Just be sincere.
- Always validate from the heart.

Crack the code of hidden feelings

Now that you know the six stages pretty well, I'll give you a secret hack into most people's everyday language. Have you noticed when you ask people how they are doing, they usually respond with common answers? Would you like to know what each answer reveals about how that person is really doing emotionally?

When you ask someone, "How are you?" these are the typical answers. Each answer reveals the stage that person might be in. Caution: Don't point this out to them (or they might become self-conscious about talking to you again). Simply use it as information to know how to direct the conversation to better love and serve them.

Remember, don't jump to conclusions, and maybe even double verify which stage they might be in by asking further questions. Or simply be extra kind, especially if you know they are hurting or having a difficult time.

I'll lay the answers out by stages so you can better see them.

Stages 1–2: "I'm fine."

Most of the time, a person is hurting so deeply and feeling like nobody cares that they try to hide that fact by saying they are "fine." If their tone of voice dips when they say "I'm fine," most likely they are not fine at all but hurting pretty deeply. The tone of voice will sound deflated or defeated. However, if the tone of voice moves up on the word "fine," they probably are just fine. If they are down in Stage 1, do your best to heartfully listen and validate to help lift them UP a little.

Stage 3 (below heart level): "I'm OK" or "I'm hangin' in there."

This is usually said with an emphatic head nod (almost as if to convince themselves they are doing OK). This is when people aren't emotionally drowning anymore, so they are OK, but they are not feeling very happy yet. They feel stable and able to handle their life, but they still feel disconnected, and their heart isn't quite in what they are doing. (As you know, they now need something to look forward to!)

Stages 4–6: "I'm good."

This is often said with a shoulder shrug. It may indicate a "shrugging off" of responsibilities, as if to say, "I'm good. No need to get any better." This is where some may get stuck in complacency because they are feeling "good." But there's so much more! Don't get complacent, my friend, at just being good. Keep moving UP until you reach full connection and that becomes your new daily reality. If you stay UP in joy and full connection, life is wonderful!

Full Connection: "Amazing!" "Fantastic!" "Glorious!" "Wonderful!" or "Life is great!"

People's answers UP here are very vibrant and joyous. They answer emphatically with a smile on their face, "I'm feeling amazing!" "Fantastic!" "Fabulous!" "Wonderful!" "Glorious!" or "Life is great, thanks!" At this fully connected level, depression is obliterated, and the state of being is joyous. Love and light flows from their hearts and eyes, and people feel amazing simply being around them. Wouldn't it be amazing to be this joyous and help lift others UP with your loving presence?

Let's explore giving REAL support

- Recognize
- Elevate
- Allow
- Love

Recognize

In order to offer support, you must first *recognize* that they are feeling low and need extra support. Be aware of those around you. When you keep yourself UP above heart-level, you live from your heart. You know you are enough, and you have an abundance of that love to give to others who are so precious to you.

Keep yourself above heart-level so you can better *recognize* when others are below heart-level. When you see/hear your family being critical or mean, take a step back and ask yourself, "How can I best support them right now?" Maybe even ask them, "How are you feeling right now?" Part of this *recognizing* is letting them see that you understand, see, and value them. This is where validation comes in. You say something like, "I can see you're having a difficult time right now. May I ask how you are feeling?" They respond, and you say something like, "Wow, that's tough. That must not feel good at all." Try to listen and validate with an understanding heart.

Elevate

Validate to *elevate!* As soon as you recognize that someone is feeling low, always *validate*.

Always reach them at the level they are currently at. If they are very low energy, try to match that with your facial expressions and tone of voice. If you're happy, cheerful, and excited, that does not match the low energy of the apathetic Stage 1. Try to match the energetic level of the situation. Sincerely try to feel what it's like for them in what they are experiencing.

And always, always be sincere with your words! This is about loving and supporting them for REAL, not just "saying all the right words" in order to get them to do what you want. This is truly seeing and loving them for who they are.

Even if you feel like you don't know how to help or what else to do, always listen to understand and then *validate*.

Allow

Ask them, "Do you still need to feel this way, or are you ready to move UP a little?" If they still need time to process that emotional charge, then *allow* them the time and space to process and heal. Sometimes that may be minutes, hours, or even days. Always *allow* them time to process. Respect their feelings and emotions. *Allow* them their choices. Yes, even I need time to process the bigger emotions, especially sadness and loss, before I try to lift myself UP again.

If they are ready to move UP a little, then ask, "May I offer a possible suggestion?" If they say, yes, only then can you offer a suggestion that matches the stage they are in. (Only offer suggestions for that stage!)

Love

Show an increase of *love* and ask, "How may I best support you?" This is different from asking, "How can I help?" Offering help suggests a one-time action. Support shows your *loving* commitment to be there for them, especially when they need you most.

Unconditionally *love* them no matter what they are experiencing or what they choose to do. Show an increase in *love*, and be available to give support when they need or ask for it. You work on keeping yourself above heart-level, and you'll be in a much better heart-space to fully *love* and support others.

Now you know how to give REAL support.

When offering support, you must always match the suggestions you offer to the stage the person is in.

Six Stages tools

Stage 6. Making progress again: Finally ready to learn the lessons, fully forgive, and celebrate the good in your life. Ready to make positive progress.

TOOL: Celebrate!

Stage 5. Feeling good: You may begin to ask, "Am I being/doing too much?" The answer is "Nope. Keep going!"

TOOL: Get physically moving out in nature.

Stage 4. Starting to feel better again: Life feels more normal. You are a lot nicer being above heart-level!

TOOL: Use your voice; ask another person for help.

Stage 3. Want to feel better: You may feel like you're in a funk, AKA not quite like yourself.

You feel more stable and able to function normally, and you are ready to feel happy again.

TOOL: Look forward to something exciting that you get to create or experience.

Stage 2. Want to want to feel better: Low energy. Lethargic. Hurting. Feeling like "nobody cares." Unhappy.

TOOL: Passive nurturing.

Stage 1. Apathetic: Zero motivation for anything. Don't want to feel better. Lie in bed or on the couch all day. Nothing could possibly make you happy, even if it's something you used to love. Feel "knocked off your feet."

Temptation: taking yourself out of the game (suicide) and possibly taking others with you (because the lie is they then won't feel the pain of you being gone because they'll be gone too). The more you listen, the more detailed these thoughts become. Don't listen to the lies!

TOOL: VALIDATE your feelings and what you are experiencing. Validate that it totally sucks to feel this low!

Stage 1 is really heavy, and it seeks to pull you down even more. Here are some tools to combat those destructive thoughts.

Tools to combat suicidal thoughts

- Say out loud, "Thank you for sharing, but I choose to live."

- Focus on one thing you DO have right NOW (something small and simple, like your finger or something ridiculous like that). Take 30 seconds and focus on what you DO have. Ready, GO!
- Focus on breathing out to relax and get more mentally present.
- Focus on breathing in to energize and get motivation to climb out of bed and have a drink of water.
- Focus on just one small next step. Now DO that step.
  - Remember the *Frozen 2* song, "Do the next right thing"? Take that advice and only focus on your next right step. You could even listen to that song to inspire you.
- As always, VALIDATE how you are feeling and what you are experiencing!

Remember, at each stage the opposing forces tempt and seek to pull you down another stage. Stage 1's temptation is to take you out of the game of life. It's tricky, because only the next step is believable to your brain. It goes both ways. Down in Stage 1, happiness isn't even believable, so just focus on going up one stage. At the top, the thought of suicide is laughable because you love your life so much you'd never want to quit.

Be aware, the temptations in your mind will try to smother hope and pull you down one stage at a time. No shame, it just is.

If you know the patterns, you can recognize these thoughts for what they really are! These thoughts of suicide and of ending this pain are simply notifications that you are in Stage 1. When you receive these "notifications," you MUST validate yourself immediately. Give yourself permission to feel what you are feeling, and recognize that it totally sucks. Give yourself that foundation to start moving up above heart-level again. You can do this!

Your life matters!!! Your feelings matter. Your thoughts matter. Your life matters. What you do every day matters. Your experiences matter. Why? Because, my friend, you matter.

Giving REAL Support

When working with yourself and others who are experiencing depression, remember this:
- Validate to lighten the weight!
- Validate to elevate!
- Validate to provide that foundation to start building yourself up again!

I've given you a lot so far. Now let's get more into what to do and what NOT to do.

Do's and don'ts of depression

Here are a few guidelines to best support yourself and people you love:

- Don't shame—that pushes depression deeper.
- Don't identify with depression. Don't say, "I am depressed." Instead say, "I am experiencing depression."
- Do love.
- Do always validate feelings.
- Don't suggest tools that are only valid in higher stages (e.g., "Just be grateful," "Just get moving and exercise," "Just choose to be happy.")
- Don't criticize.
- Never give up; keep going!
- Don't tell the person "I know how you feel," because you very well may not. It could feel devalidating when you phrase it like that. Simply say, "That must feel_____." (If you guess wrong, it's OK. They see you are trying to understand, and they may correct you by telling you specifically what they are feeling.)
- Don't push loved ones away. Don't exclude them from activities or from being around you just because they are acting depressed.

- Do keep healthy boundaries.
- Do include them.
- Do unconditionally show love.
- Do allow them time and space to heal.
- Do ask, "How may I best support you?"
- Do ask, "Do you still need time to process and feel this way, or are you ready to move up a little?"

If necessary, remind others, "It's OK to feel like you are feeling. Please use caution with the actions you choose. Feeling angry is separate from angrily punching someone in the face. It's OK and safe to feel; it's not OK to harm yourself or another person."

A quick note on medical support

Please always be super-supportive of those who need and use medications. Remember that shame only depresses further. There is no shame in getting help when you need it. Please be loving, kind, and understanding of those who need that medical support.

If or when you do use medications, remember that the body was designed to heal itself physically. However, it wasn't designed to heal itself emotionally. You must choose emotional healing. Your body will heal a cut, but you must choose to forgive others and choose healing for your heart.

If the body wasn't designed to heal emotions, then what are we supposed to do? If you get antidepressants that are designed to numb/ease the pain, you still must work on healing those emotions in addition to that medical support. Pain-numbing pills work best when the body can then proceed to heal itself without feeling the pain. However, depression is often more of a mental or emotional problem than a physical one. If you are using medications to support yourself, realize that you must still heal yourself mentally or emotionally as well. Once you heal yourself mentally and emotionally, you might find some "crutches" unnecessary. Your doctor may then choose to adjust your medical support as needed.

I'm not the expert, but some things may lessen for you, and some things may forever need that medical support. This is why you must work with your doctor to make these critical medical decisions.

Do happiness tools really work?

While learning about happiness, the number-one question a lot of people have is "What happiness tools actually work?" The answer is all of them. You just have to know when to use them, how to use them, and who to use them with.

I have a friend who is a very deep emotional processor. His family didn't realize he'd been experiencing depression for many months because he's usually quiet anyway. He tried using affirmations and other empowerment tools (you'll learn more of these in my other books), but he said they "didn't work." He seemed to reject the self-mastery world for a while because the tools didn't help him feel better.

What was the problem: Do empowerment tools really not work? Or was he trying to use them in the wrong stage?

Empowerment tools such as Affirmations, Vision Boards, Power Poses, etc., are amazing, and I use them every day. However, if you try to jump from Stage 1 (apathetic and numb) to Stage 4 (happy, connected, and above heart-level), it won't work. You must use tools that help you get through the stage you are currently at. You must set your foundation through validation and self-nurture before you even try to use empowerment tools. Empowerment tools work best when you are at least above heart-level. Your heart energy must be on before you can add energy and power to it. Does this make sense?

Do happiness tools work? Yes, you just have to know exactly when and how to use them.

Here are a few examples:

Happiness tools arranged by stages

Stage 1:
- VALIDATE!
- Listen unconditionally: seek to understand and validate feelings.

Stage 2:
- Passively nurture.
- Watch a funny video to smile a little.
- Get a massage.
- Listen to uplifting music or podcasts.
- Eat supportive, healthy foods. Get more B vitamins.
  - Truly a master in the health arena whom I greatly trust, Dr. Roland Phillips, advises that for depression, "The biggest component biochemically is a B vitamin deficiency. See a practitioner that can order Standard Process supplements."

Stage 3:
- Look forward to creating or experiencing something you will enjoy.

Stage 4:
- Ask for help.
- Talk to someone who will listen, offer love and support, and suggest possible solutions.

Stage 5:
- Exercise.
- Physically get moving.
- Get out in nature.

Stage 6:
- This is the only stage where you can "Look on the bright side."
- This is the ONLY STAGE where you can use this phrase on yourself:
  - "When life gives you melons—wait, lemons—make lemonade."
- Feel gratitude.
- Learn the lessons.
- Be grateful for who you have become through this process.
- Celebrate! (Use this highest, most sincere form of gratitude.)
- Keep moving forward.

Congratulations! You've read this far. You're probably feeling a little lighter and more hopeful.

Tiny action

- Recognize where a loved one is emotionally at right now. Ask them, "How may I best support you?"

- Now give them unconditional, loving support in a REAL way.

Give yourself a high five and say, "I love myself, I live above heart-level, and I offer people REAL support."

The UNdepressed Heart

UNDERSTANDING FAWPA

Fear, Anxiety, Worry, and Panic Attacks

"Anxiety actually signifies that there is a part of us in need of attention and/or support."
~ John Crawford

"There's nothing to be anxious about. Just snap out of it." If you've ever heard that, you know IT DOESN'T HELP! You know that it's ridiculous to be afraid, but you FEEL extremely anxious and afraid during the anxiety/panic attack. Am I right?

Andrew Solomon, in his TED Talk "Depression: The Secrets We Share," describes anxiety and panic attacks something like this: You feel fearful even though there's nothing to be afraid of. As the panic hits, you may even think, "This is ridiculous," but you are still curled up in a ball feeling extremely anxious. You're afraid and panicked, but you don't really know why.

An anxiety attack usually comes as a trigger response to a stressor. Something triggering happens (or something stressful and worrisome comes to mind, and you may follow the downward spiral of thoughts/emotions), and your thoughts, emotions, and entire being are completely overtaken by the anxiety. It feels kind of like being "brain hijacked."

Similar, yet quite different, is the panic attack. What happens during a panic attack is (and correct me if I'm wrong) something sends a "misstep" signal to your brain. Normally, if you miss the last step on the stairs, you get a sinking feeling in your stomach. It doesn't feel good, but since you know logically why you felt that (I missed the last step), your brain calms down and says, "Everything's OK because I know why we felt that."

However, during a panic attack, you feel that misstep feeling (for whatever unknown reason), and since your brain doesn't know why you're feeling that, it goes into hyperaware mode looking for the reason. Since there is no visible logical reason, your brain goes into hyper-active-aware-mode feeling like, "What is about to happen?" You know how you get a sinking feeling right before something bad is about to happen, and you hyperfocus on what bad thing might happen to try and avoid it? During a panic attack, you feel that misstep feeling, your brain sees no known reason for it, so it panics and becomes hyperaware, trying to find the reason. Since you can't see it, the panic deepens and you start to freak out because you feel like some unknown terrible thing is about to happen. Terrified, you may curl up in a ball, totally freaked out until the panic goes away. Now I've never personally felt that, but it would be terrifying to feel that way!

Baseline, if you have a loved one or friend who experiences panic attacks, please don't say unhelpful and hurtful things like, "What's wrong with you? Just snap out of it. You're being ridiculous. There's nothing to panic over." Just lovingly understand that they know it's ridiculous, but their brain is freaking out, and they legitimately feel terrified.

I'll be honest, I've never experienced an anxiety or panic attack in my life. That is probably true for most people. This is exactly why it's extremely difficult for those who do deal with anxiety and panic attacks. Most people don't understand since they've never experienced it. Well-meaning friends and loved ones say, "Just snap out of it," but that always makes it worse because it adds shame on top of the anxiety. They might say, "You SHOULD be able to handle this. What's wrong with you?" HELLO!! Words like that only hurt people more!

Understanding and awareness are the first steps toward progression. You or a loved one may always deal with this anxiety, or it may lessen as time goes on, but know this: You are amazing and loved. Your feelings are valid, and you can handle this!

What about anxiety?

"I lost my wallet!" I frantically began to search for it everywhere. "Did I lose it on our last trip? Did someone just steal it? What am I going to do now?" As I'm writing this, that literally just happened yesterday, and it's not a good feeling when you lose something that you need!

Whatever the trigger, anxiety doesn't feel good at all. It feels like a constant worry about the unknown. It's basically hyperactive worrying. Worse yet is when you feel like you couldn't handle what may happen, and the anxiety increases.

That day I lost my wallet, anxiety totally hijacked all my thoughts and emotions. It was difficult to focus on anything else. I had planned to sit down and work on writing this book for a few hours that day, but I definitely wasn't above heart-level. I was so distracted by this anxiety.

Not to devalidate my own experience, but some of you may be thinking, "That's it? That's what you were worried about? That's no big deal." Unfortunately, that's how many people dealing with anxiety seem to be treated, like, "What's wrong with you. You should be able to handle this." Remember, "shoulds" shame, and shame depresses.

In the midst of this overwhelming anxiety, I knew what I needed to do: the Fear-to-Funny technique. My brilliant husband created this tool to help his high-end clients overcome their fears (specifically illogical fears). When our children have a nightmare, he uses this with them too. If our child wakes up feeling very afraid, Eric helps them through the process of drawing out their fear and changing it. They laugh and giggle at the new image. Our child feels validated, loved, and safe, and then falls back asleep peacefully. Every time.

Have you ever been afraid of something that you knew was ridiculous, but you felt the fear anyway? Fears must be addressed. If you try to run away from your fears, they chase you and get bigger. If you ignore or avoid your fears, they may turn into the subconscious realm of fear more commonly known as anxiety. Anxiety shows up as a vague fear. You're fearful, but you may not know exactly why. If you ignore your fears, or you're so fearful about something that you're unwilling to face it, it will manifest itself as anxiety (an unconscious fear).

One tool to help lessen these fears is the Fear-to-Funny technique:

Frightened, Ashley ran into our room and woke her daddy up. In her nightmare, large man-eating slugs were coming to attack her if she breathed in at all. Eric immediately got a pen and paper and asked her to draw it out. He had her turn the drawing into something funny. She then looked at her drawing, added a few more details and laughed, saying, "Oh, that's just long-nosed ladybugs coming to play with me! That can't harm me!"

She's never mentioned that nightmare again. It was rewritten in her brain, and the emotional charge of the fear was totally gone. Let's do this now so you better understand how to use this.

Fear-to-Funny Technique:
- Get a piece of paper and a pen or pencil.
- Write down something you are either anxious about or fearing.
- Draw a visual representation of that fear.
- Now look at your drawing and turn it into something humorous. Draw on top of the old picture and transform it into something

funny. (It helps if you laugh out loud once you see the "funny" in your drawing.)
- Say out loud, "Oh, that's just_____(describe what the new drawing is). That can't harm me."

This (1) validates your fear, and (2) changes that emotional charge from fear into laughter.

After I did this Fear-to-Funny, I felt a lot of the anxiety lighten and calm down. It wasn't totally overtaking my thoughts and emotions anymore. I was still feeling very concerned and uncertain, but it was a bit easier to handle.

The next step I used to combat this anxiety was to write out a list of what I could control. What could I do to lessen the impact and start to make it right again?

Losing my wallet:
- Check my bank accounts to make sure nobody's been spending on my debit and credit cards.
- Go to the DLD and get a new driver's license.
- Pause all my bankcard accounts/ask for reissue of these cards.
- Look all around for my wallet one more time.
- Pray for guidance.
- Make a list of what I can focus on doing today.

This helped me realize that in the worst-case scenario (I never find my wallet), there are actions I could take to be able to handle this situation. In the best case, I would be extremely glad if or when I found it again.

Our family's motto is "Prepare for the worst, but expect the BEST!" This helps you realize you could handle whatever may come. At the same time, you put all your mental and emotional energy toward creating what you DO want. Either way, you're prepared for your future.

When hit with uncertainty and facing the unknown, the best attitude to take is "I can handle this." While out at the park, I recently heard a mother tell her children, "You can do hard things." I tell this to you now too: you can do hard things.

Life was not designed to be easy—coasting and "easy" only go downhill. Progress and everything worth going after in life are always uphill. Becoming better is moving UP. So when life is difficult, remember these few things: You CAN handle it. You CAN do difficult things. You are stronger than you know.

Now say to yourself, "If I can get through this, I can get through anything!" My friend, you are loved, cared for, and extremely valuable and precious. You are totally worth it.

Now, let's unpack all these fear words.

Understanding FAWPA

Fear: Conscious anticipation of discomfort/pain.
- Logical fear: there's a logical reason to feel afraid (i.e., a tiger is about to pounce on you).
- Illogical fear: you are in a safe environment, yet you fear discomfort/pain that may or may not actually happen. (People might tell you, "There's no reason to be afraid," yet you feel afraid anyway.)

Anxiety: Unconscious fear (not consciously aware of what you are actually fearing). Fear of the unknown. Feeling uncertain.

Worry: Prolonged fear. Fear is now a habit.

Panic **A**ttack: As explained earlier, something trips the "misstep" feeling within you, but you don't know why. Your brain hijacks control and prepares you for the worst. It feels terrifying.

Understanding FAWPA

Whatever the cause for you feeling fear, anxiety, worry, or panic, please realize your thoughts and feelings are valid simply because you really are feeling that way! Once you validate your feelings, you can begin to build your foundation for addressing your fears in a more supportive way.

The self-mastery world says, "Awareness is the first step toward change."

What you can see, you can change. If you can see your fears and worries for what they are, you can change them. Your first step is to create a "worry list."

Worry List

Right now, write out a list of everything you are worried or fearful about.

I'll get you started.

- I feel worried about …
- I'm afraid that …
- I'm avoiding …
- I feel like I can't handle …
- I'm so scared of …
- I'll never be able to …
- I can't do what I want because …
- If I_____, people will …

Now, crumple up your worry list and throw it away. Choose to let go of some of that fear/anxiety. It may not all go away, but at least you can lessen the intensity and start focusing on something you can do.

Tips to Lessen Worry and Anxiety

- "Name it to tame it" (thanks to Generationmindful.com for this phrase!). Name what you are feeling to lessen its effect on you.
- Rate it on a scale of 1 to 10. This switches you from the emotional brain into the logical side of your brain. Since anxiety and worry tend to be more illogical fears, this will help lessen their effect when you switch to the logical side of your brain.
- Face the fear head-on. Tell yourself you CAN handle it. Action helps dispel fear because then you know you CAN do it!
- Breathe deeply and evenly to bring yourself back to the present moment and reconnect to yourself. Try this now!
  - Rhythmic breathing: Breathe in - 2 - 3 - 4, hold it in - 2 - 3 - 4, breathe out - 2 - 3 - 4, hold it out - 2 - 3 - 4, breathe in - 2 - 3 - 4 … and continue for another minute.

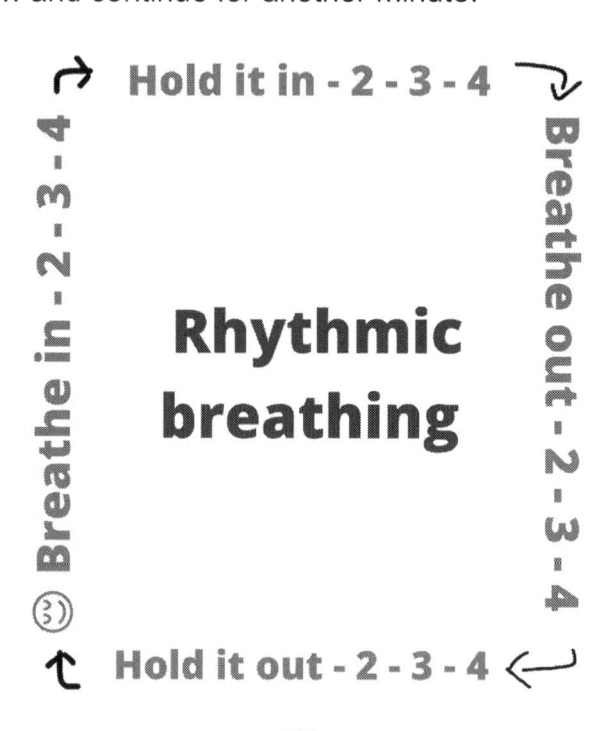

Rhythmic breathing

Breathe in - 2 - 3 - 4
Hold it in - 2 - 3 - 4
Breathe out - 2 - 3 - 4
Hold it out - 2 - 3 - 4

Understanding FAWPA

Fear/worry/anxiety don't feel very good, do they? It's because you are expecting to experience discomfort and pain! What if it were possible to slightly change your perspective so you began to anticipate feeling good? Fear and excitement are closely related. Look at this:

Fear = anticipation of discomfort/pain
Excitement = anticipation of pleasure

If you are anticipating something you are about to do as uncomfortable/painful, you will be experiencing fear. You may prolong the fear, and then it turns into worry. Or you may be so fearful about something that you're unwilling to face it, and it manifests itself as anxiety (an unconscious fear).

On the flip side, you may start to look forward to experiencing more good things in your life. It may not be easy, but it is possible. It's worth shifting your perspective so you can feel better. Begin to anticipate more pleasure and good things in your life! Look forward to doing more of what you enjoy!

Remember, when you're dealing with any parts of FAWPA, it doesn't feel good. Yet, your feelings and concerns are very valid, and you are worth doing something about these concerns.

You're not broken. You don't need fixing. You are experiencing something difficult, and you just need support. You need validation and REAL support to help you work through these experiences. Life is excruciatingly difficult sometimes, and we must rally together to help us all move up and out of these deeply hurtful and dark experiences. We can do this. We are here on earth together for a reason: to love, serve, and support. We're not meant to be alone in our difficulties.

You may deal with these difficult emotions a lot. Some things never go away for good, but would it be helpful if you could lessen their effects on you? Or maybe get through these experiences more quickly? (In other words, depression lasting hours or days, rather than months or years.)

I'm so grateful that many online/in-person communities exist where women can go to be understood by others who have had similar experiences. Lonely is a world where you are the only one who understands what you are dealing with, especially in the arena of mental-emotional health! Only recently is this being better understood by professionals and the general public. I'm glad this world is fast progressing in supporting mental-emotional health!

My vision is that depression, anxiety, and panic attacks can be more understood so that people will more lovingly assist and validate. Rather than shaming others and pushing them away with rude and hurtful comments, I envision people allowing others to work through their experiences. They unconditionally love and validate, showing that the other person's feelings and emotions are valid. They communicate that no matter what actions others take, they are valid, valuable, loved human beings. All people deserve love, consideration, and to be heard. This helps others feel understood, valid, and valued. Every person on this earth is extremely valuable and very precious. This includes you, my friend.

If you've ever been hurt by someone's unknowing comments, let's spread this message of hope, validation, and love, so that fewer people will ever have to experience that again. If you are at a high enough stage (3 or above), find it in your heart to forgive all those people who mistreated and misjudged you.

If you're not ready for that yet, validate your feelings. Allow yourself to feel what you are feeling, and know that those are totally valid feelings. It is OK for you to feel that way. Remember to find ways to nurture and passively care for yourself first.

I always tell my kids, "It is OK to feel that way. What's not OK is when you act from those negative emotions and hurt yourself or someone else." For example, it is totally OK to feel angry. If you feel so, please do! What's not OK is to hit or hurt someone. Whether angry or not, it is never OK to physically, mentally, or emotionally hurt someone else (or yourself!).

Validate and process through your own emotions; let the storm of emotion pass through you. Use emotional processing tools like journaling, finishing the conversation, yelling, and throwing a tantrum (while alone!). When that emotional storm calms, it is then later OK to ask permission, share your feelings with the other person, and tell them that what they did was not OK.

Example: If you're feeling infuriatingly frustrated with your husband, don't yell and nag. Instead, process your emotions by yourself. Later, when your emotions have calmed, that's when you go back and ask permission to share your feelings with him. Lead your discussion with the intention of finding a possible solution. Make sure the new solution is a win-win for both of you. If either of you are highly charged with negative emotion, that is NOT the time to try to solve problems (unless you want to aggravate and create a bigger problem).

My friend, your emotions are valid. Your feelings are valid. Allow yourself to healthfully process your emotions. When that emotional storm has passed, that's when you can discuss feelings and seek possible solutions. You've got this!

Tiny action

- Lessen the intensity of one of your fears by using the Fear-to-Funny technique.

- Write a "worry list," then tear it up and throw it away.

Give yourself a high five and say, "I love myself. I love and validate other people!"

The UNdepressed Heart

GRIEF AND GUIDANCE

"We're here for a reason. I believe a bit of the reason is to throw little torches out to lead people through the dark."
~ Whoopi Goldberg

Shocked, I couldn't believe what my husband had just told me. We'd only finally found her two years ago, and now she was gone. I cried for days. Eric was numb with shock and disbelief. My heart tore apart because he'd searched for so many years to find her, and now … Then I thought of my children. Ashley was so excited to have a "#3 Grandma." How could I tell her she's now gone? My heart was completely broken—crushed. I did nothing but cry. It was too much. I called others to talk, but they just didn't seem to understand my grief. They thought, "Why are you so sad, Heather? It's not like you knew her very well." Does that matter? She's my dear husband's birth-mother and my children's grandmother, and now we'll never get to see her again.

Throughout the grieving process, I felt alone because Eric was going through his own deep grief. My friends and family around me didn't know or didn't really understand me and my pain. I dreaded telling my young children, so we just didn't say anything about it to them for a long time. I couldn't stand to see how it would affect them. That would have been too much for me.

Loss of any kind can hurt us deeply. It's extremely important to understand the different ways people process grief to support ourselves and our loved ones through this excruciatingly painful time. Remember, all people process grief and pain differently. Many people go through similar patterns, but it never looks the same between two people. We are all unique, and we all process grief and painful loss in our own individual ways.

Here are the basics of a few popular grief-cycle models. Let's get an overview of the possible grief phases you or a loved one may go through.

The Bowlby and Parkes model

Possible feelings in each stage include:

Shock and numbness
- Emotions are overwhelming. Shock. Denial. Physical distress. Hurts so deep you just go numb. Going numb helps you to survive and not have too much to process all at once. This is a necessary and valid stage of grief.

Yearning and searching
- Searching for comfort to fill the void created by this major loss. Yearning for that connection to still be there. Preoccupied with the loss.

Despair and disorganization
- Questioning. Feeling angry. Realizing that the loss is permanent. Difficulty even thinking about the future because who/what you lost won't ever be there again. Hard to find hope. Feeling aimless. Seeking solitude to process the pain.

Reorganization and recovery
- Hope in healing the mind and heart. Sadness and longing never truly go away, but we can begin to heal and reconnect with others to support and love us. Begin to find your "new normal."

The Kübler-Ross model basics (with her newer additions)

Shock and Denial
- Deeply profound feelings.
- Facts seem unbelievable.
- Tragic and unexpected loss can cause disbelief and deep shock.
- Numbness.
- Denial: "That can't be true; there must be a mistake." "That didn't happen." "This isn't permanent."
- Feeling paralyzed emotionally.
- Feel physically ill, nausea, increased heart rate, and/or trouble sleeping.
- It feels totally unbelievable.

Shame and Pain
- Feelings of pain, sadness, regret, and emotional suffering.
- Feelings of disbelief and shock may lessen, and feelings of shame and pain come in.
- Feel shame of, "If only …" "I should have …" "Why am I the one still alive," "It's all my fault."
- "Why didn't I …" "If only I could tell them …"
- Pain and regrets hurt deeply: these are natural grieving emotions. It's important to process through and allow yourself to feel what you are experiencing because it is very real to you.
- Healthfully processing your experience is critical to finding healing.

Anger and Bargaining
- Feel anger and frustration.
- Snappy: feel like a "time bomb" about to explode at any moment.
- Blame others for the loss.
- Try to reverse permanent loss with "bargaining" or "making a deal."

Processing your emotions in a healthy way:
- Remember, it is 100% OK to feel what you are feeling. However, it is never OK to harm another person because of how you are feeling. You can feel angry, but it's not OK to mentally, emotionally, or physically hurt someone (including yourself) just because you are angry. Be angry and upset, just don't hurt anyone.

Depression, Loneliness, and Reflection
- More crying/sobbing as realization comes that the loss is irreversible.
- Changes in eating and sleeping habits may occur.
- Unexplained physical pains like headaches or stomachaches, sore muscles.
- Feeling the heaviness of the loss.
- Isolation and loneliness.
- Can sink into Stage 1 depression, feeling apathetic and unable to even move.
- Withdraw to try to deal with this grief alone.
- Personal reflection.

The Upward Turn
- Loss is still felt, and you begin to handle these grief symptoms a little better.
- Feel a little more hopeful about the future again.
- Feel more peace and acceptance.

Testing
- Search for ways to cope with this grief.
- Try new things to help support you in this grief.
- Look for real-life solutions to bring back some sense of normalcy to your life.

Reconstruction and Working Through
- Emotions settle, and mental strain begins to calm.
- Easier to process emotions and seek solutions to managing grief and life.
- May begin to set goals for the future. Start to rebuild your life.
- Start to have a sense of control in your life again.
- Taking care of yourself seems less daunting than before.

Can you see how the stages of grief parallel the stages of depression in a lot of ways? If you are grieving and feel totally numb, apathetic, and in denial, you are down in Stage 1 depression as well, and the best thing you can do is to recognize and validate what you are experiencing to help lift you up. Always allow yourself time to process, and always give yourself that foundation of validation to help you start rebuilding your life again.

Acceptance and Hope
- Emotions may still be unpredictable.
- You may begin to feel more acceptance of what now is.
- Find hope in looking forward again.
- Begin to rebuild your life again and find a new normal.

Here's one last perspective that may help you better understand what you or a loved one may experience.

The Tonkin model: Growing around grief

Instead of saying that grief lessens and goes away after a time, Dr. Lois Tonkin believes that it's an all-consuming feeling that never really goes away. Many people learn to adapt and grow themselves around that grief, essentially creating a "new normal."

How to best support someone through the grieving process

First, understand that everyone processes grief differently. Realize this may take a long time, and the emptiness and sadness felt will never completely go away, especially when grieving the loss of a loved one.

- Don't try to make it better by "fixing" it.
- Don't try to make them laugh or smile if they are not ready. (Wait until they are in at least Stage 3 before trying to "cheer them up.")
- Give them space and time to heal.
- Love and support them unconditionally.
- Be available to talk if and when they are ready.
- Never push or "should" them.
- Listen with an understanding heart.
- Meet them at the stage they are at, and only offer help or advice that is appropriate for that stage.
- When in doubt, always validate!

Grief can come from losing a loved one to death, distance, or a relationship disconnection. It can come from job or lifestyle loss. It can come from growing up and "losing" your childhood. It can come from losing physical objects. It can even come from losing a dream that you never turned into a reality. However it comes, grief is real and valid in all its forms. It always "counts."

While grieving, you may experience only parts of these proposed cycles. You may go back and forth between a couple of stages. It's never clear-cut, and it can feel quite unpredictable. Allow yourself to feel whatever you are experiencing, and find ways to healthfully cope and process.

This will never look the same between two people. I've shown you some patterns to see if you recognize anything you may be experiencing. Hopefully this helps you feel more understood and validated. It is 100% OK to grieve and feel all the emotions that go with it. Even if you're the only one around you, it's OK to feel and experience these emotions. You are valid and you are loved. Please realize you are not alone in this. Many people do understand something similar to what you are going through to at least a small degree. You will eventually get through this and be OK again (even if you don't see it yet).

This takes time. Realize things will never be the same again. You will be changed, and eventually you will find a new "normal." Hopefully you will learn the lessons and become stronger and maybe even more compassionate to others experiencing loss as well.

Help is always available, especially when deep grief is making it hard to function and live life at all. Before it becomes too debilitating for you, reach out for help in any way that you can. There is no "wrong" way to grieve, but you must make sure you are processing that grief in healthy ways.

If a loved one or you are experiencing extreme difficulty, we can connect you with a licensed practitioner who specializes in helping people up through deep depression, often at no cost. Please email office@FeelWellLiveWell.com with the subject line "Treatment." Please include your phone number so they can contact you to see how they can best support you.

There is always hope and help for you, my friend.

Why do we experience difficult things?

"Nothing in life has happened to you. It's happened for you. Every disappointment. Every wrong. Even every closed door has helped make you into who you are."
~ Joel Osteen

Our experiences shape our soul. Maybe, just maybe, our feelings of deep grief, sorrow, and hurt somehow prepare us to feel greater joy. After experiencing the deepest, darkest moment in his life, the great missionary Alma exclaimed, "My soul was filled with joy as exceeding as was my pain!"

The depths of sorrows you feel make room for you to feel the exquisite joys God has in store for you. If you grieve deeply over losing a loved one, imagine the depths of your joy when you are reunited in the world to come.

Have you ever lost something important to you, and you were devastated? Then when you found it, you felt overjoyed! The sadder you were at the loss, the greater the joy when it was restored unto you.

Imagine God as the potter and you as the clay. He is molding and shaping you into a powerful vessel for good. You feel pokes and prods that push you down into the depths of your soul. This creates a void, a space, in which He can then fill you with joy and goodness. If the potter didn't push holes into the clay, how then could the pot be useful for containing anything good? There would be no room; it would still just be a lump of clay.

God uses the depths of our sorrows to prepare us for the exquisite joys He has in store for us. You may not see it yet, but someday all your experiences will come together for your good.

> Only remind someone of this if they are in Stage 6 or above—you aren't ready to "learn the lesson" or "look on the bright side" until you are above heart-level, reconnected with self, others, and nature. Learning the lesson and feeling gratitude for your experiences connects you back with God/the Divine. You must be ready in order to learn those lessons and feel that gratitude for who you are becoming through all your experiences.

Coping Strategies to Deal with Grief

Grieving brings many ups and downs, yet there are ways to process and begin to heal. Your life won't be the same, but you can heal and begin to create your "new normal."

Healthy grief processing
Grieving loss of any sort can be very difficult. Here are a few possible ideas to help you process in a healthy way.

- Journaling.
- Talking to someone you know who cares about you.
- Seeking professional help.
- Taking steps to move through the six stages of depression.
- Allowing yourself to feel and validate your experiences.

- Giving yourself time and space to process and begin to heal.
- Recognizing you are not alone.

"Finish the conversation" tool: When alone, state (out loud) all that you are feeling and experiencing. Get it all out. If necessary, "finish the conversation" with the person you need to speak to that isn't present. Tell them everything you wish to say to them. (Hint: It must be spoken out loud to help it process and get it out of your mind.)

Possible notebook prompts:
- I feel sad because …
- I feel alone because …
- I feel devastated because …
- Things will never be the same because …
- Some possible things I can do to cope today are …
- If I could tell that person what's on my heart, I would say …
- I am feeling …

Your experience is no less valid just because it may be different from someone else's experience. Your feelings are totally valid. You are valid.

Tiny action

- Pick one notebook prompt from above and fill it out.

Give yourself a hug and say, "I am loved, and I am cared for."

BUILDING BETTER RELATIONSHIPS

"Shared joy is a double joy; shared sorrow is half a sorrow."
~ Anonymous

"Just stop that right now!" I totally messed up. I was overbearing with my sweet child, and he emotionally went deep internally and ran away into the other room. As soon as I recognized my mistake, I went to him and sincerely apologized. His face calmed and brightened a little. He gave me a sweet hug, and then went off happily to play.

Forgiveness and apologies

Forgiving quickly is an essential attribute. Frequent apologizing and forgiving builds strong relationships. Let's face it, we all make stupid, hurtful mistakes sometimes. We will always be imperfect, but we can always quickly apologize.

I teach my children the four steps to an apology. I know this will influence them positively for the rest of their lives.

My younger son is a deep internal processor. He feels things very intensely and very deeply. I know if he can get in the habit of quick apologies and being quick to forgive, he will be a much happier and more well-balanced adult. I have seen too many adults with his similar personality out of balance. They are the silent yet very emotionally unreachable (angry) men that many people tend to avoid.

He also has a very happy, fun, and silly side. I know it shines more when he processes his emotions in a healthy way. His immediate response to the negative is to run away into another room to process his emotions. He doesn't like it if he has intentionally or accidentally hurt someone. If he ever hurts me, he runs away to be by himself to process his emotions. He needs that space. When he is ready, he always comes back and apologizes to me. He then returns to being happy and playful again. If he didn't have the four-step apology as a tool, I have no idea how long he'd be deep down in his own emotions. And he's only four! (Yes, his future wife can thank me now.)

Four steps to a sincere apology
- "Just now I …" (State what you did.)
- "That wasn't OK." (This acknowledges and validates the fact that it wasn't OK.)
- "I apologize."
- "Will you please forgive me?" (Now, strive to be better and never do that thing again.)

Yes, that intro story was my own. I wish I was a perfect mother, but I'm not there yet. After recognizing my mistake, I remorsefully said to my son, "Christopher, just now I spoke meanly to you. That wasn't OK. I apologize. Will you please forgive me?"

Pro tip: The other person has total choice to forgive immediately or not. Either way, you've done your part in asking for forgiveness. I tell my kids they can respond to an apology with "Not yet," or "Yes, I forgive you."

A sincere four-step apology will turn the heart back on because it is very similar to repenting. The Four Rs of Repentance are Recognize,

Remorse, Reconcile with the person, and Recommit to being better. Going through the entire repentance process will release you from that minor guilt. Remember, shame is the counterfeit, and it tries to get you to hide from your mistakes. Guilt is that internal nudge inspiring you to repent and make it right again.

Repentance is simply a course correction. If you desire to be happy, course-correct quickly and live more from your heart. This helps you realign with your true self.

Four Rs of repentance:
- Recognize.
- Feel Remorse.
- Reconcile: make it right.
- Recommit to being better.

Remember the four steps to forgiveness?

Morter steps of forgiveness:
- Recognize your own fault and forgive yourself.
- Forgive the other person completely.
- Ask and allow them to forgive you (for you holding on to this negative emotion and directing it back at them).
- See the good and learn the lesson.

Do you notice how these three groups have similar patterns? In order to free yourself emotionally from these anchors that hold you down, you must learn to quickly apologize. I seriously apologize to my husband and children at least five times every day (yes, I'm human and imperfect, just like most people). The other side of apologies is forgiveness. The quicker you forgive, the faster you are going to feel better and the healthier you will be. Trust me. If stuck emotions block healing, then forgiveness allows healing. Forgiveness heals because it removes the blockages and allows your body to heal itself (as it was divinely created to do).

My daily personal mantra is "I immediately apologize, and I am quick to forgive."

Helping my children feel better—dealing with "big" emotions

It's tough seeing our children get hurt or feel angry, sad, lonely, and all the unpleasant human feelings and emotions. When they get hurt, it hurts our mommy hearts. We wish we could immediately make it all better, don't we?

However, we can't always make it better. Many times our children simply need more time to process these "big" emotions.

When these "big" emotions do come, I remind my children, "It's OK to feel how you are feeling. It's not OK to hurt someone else just because you're feeling that. Feeling angry is different than angrily hitting someone. It's OK and safe to feel; it is not OK to hurt yourself or another person."

I always give them time and space to process their emotions. Remember the REAL support? With my children, I always ask, "Do you still need more time to feel that way, or are you ready to do something to feel better?"

When you ask your children this, always honor their answer. Sometimes people really do need more time to process and feel the way they are feeling. Allow them that space. Later you can ask them again if they still need to feel that way, or if they are ready to start feeling better again. This validates the fact that sometimes we do need more time to process emotions. If something majorly emotionally upsetting just happened, let that emotional storm run its course.

After the "storm" has settled, ask if they are ready to want to feel better again.

Sometimes people just need to cry a bit more, but sometimes people are ready to change right then. How do you know? You simply ask.

Helping children deal with disappointment

"It's almost here!" We hyped up Ashley's special 8th birthday for more than a year! We planned a weeklong birthday trip to Disneyworld for just the three of us (Eric, me, and Ashley). As the oldest of our five children, that's a big deal for her! Eric reserved dining with all of Ashley's favorite characters. She would get a fabulous princess makeover. It was going to be amazing!

But then March 2020 hit. Suddenly the whole world closed down for two weeks. Weeks of lockdown turned into months. We soon realized we wouldn't be able to take her for her special birthday trip that we'd promised her. My heart nearly broke. We procrastinated telling Ashley the change of plans because we didn't want to disappoint her.

Eric and I discussed it together, and we figured out a win-win way to approach her. We said, "Ashley, we know you're aware of what is going on in the world right now. Your birthday is in a few weeks, and it's a possibility that the world will still be closed down. What are some possible solutions?" We asked her, "How can we say, 'Give me this, or something better?'" We told her we'd still take her on her birthday trip, whether it was later this year or the next year. Maybe then it would be even better (especially since she'd be taller next year—tall enough to ride the largest roller coaster there)! As a backup plan, she said she'd look forward to going to a nickel arcade for her actual birthday.

April 29th came, and every fun possibility remained closed. We did the best we could with a special birthday at home. Hilariously, my husband ordered a men's Cinderella costume. I did his hair, makeup, and splashed on extra sparkles. Eric rang the doorbell on Ashley's birthday morning as "DadZinkerbell." She thought that was too funny. He even held a "princess tea party" with her. (The things a daddy will do to give his daughter a smile :) We did our best with what we had, and we had the attitude of, "Give me this or something better."

Whenever you're looking forward to something, always say, "Please give me this, or something better." This is what I do with my Vision Board goals. Wouldn't it be amazing to get what you desire or something even better? Have a flexible enough attitude to truly believe you will either receive this great gift or something even better!

Ashley still felt disappointed about not going on her special trip, but she wasn't devastated. She had the "give me this or something better" attitude, so she still had something to look forward to on her birthday. She also knows we keep our promises, so she will get an even better birthday trip with mommy and daddy soon!

When disappointment hits, trust that things will always work out in your favor. Trust that God will give you something better; He always turns tragedies and sorrows into something much better. Always. You may not understand now, but maybe one day you'll look back and see God's wisdom in every part of your life.

Stay above heart-level

The best way to build relationships is by building yourself up first. When you love yourself more, then you can love others more. You can't fill others with an empty cup. You can't effectively love others with a disconnected heart. When your goal is to keep yourself above heart-level as much as possible, your relationships will become better and stronger.

Here's a great way to connect with others at a heart-level:

Heart-to-heart hugs!

Most people block their heart when they hug other people. Let's change this. Let's connect with others at a deeper level. When you hug someone, turn to the right so that your heart (on the left side) lines up with their heart. This connects you at that heart-level and strengthens your relationship. This helps each other feel loved, safe, and truly cared for. Try it! Give someone in your family a heart-to-heart hug for at least 20 seconds every day. See what a difference that makes!

Now let's get into what NOT to do in relationships!

Gossip and Criticism: Harmful, hurtful; avoid them like the plague!

"Gosh, Heather, what do you think of that new girl? Can you believe she does everything wrong?" I responded, "I don't know. I haven't worked with her much." My co-worker continued, "Oh, well, she ... blah, blah, blah ..." (Snap!) I tried to stay out of the gossip, but I guess I said the wrong thing. She then tried to "fill me in" on the details of why she didn't like this other girl. The problem with me taking that approach of "I don't know" was that she still kept gossiping. Luckily, I've learned better. I now know when it comes to gossip, just say, "No comment."

Gossip

Gossip = talking negatively about a person who is not present.

It is extremely hurtful! You'll never know the wide-ranging effects of the critical judgments you spread about others. Remember, gossip was exactly what threw me deep into Stage 1 depression. It cut my heart so deep. That was the deepest, darkest time of my life. It took me a long time to recover, and that was just one comment from one person!

My friend, please be kind. Please be aware of others. If you must say something critical about someone else, just don't. You always have the option to say nothing. If you must get it out of you, write it all down, then destroy the paper! Get that emotion and energetic charge out of you by writing those hurtful words down. Then destroy those words and show your mind who's really in charge. You are completely in charge of the words you use.

Words are power tools. You can use them to build up or destroy. You can tear someone down or you can lift them UP with the words you choose. Make it a habit to lift yourself UP every day with the words you use, and it will be much easier to build up others too. Words have meaning. Words have creation energy. Words truly do have a "more powerful effect than the sword." Use your words wisely.

Let's have our goal be to build people up with our words and inspire those around us to live above heart-level as well. Can you imagine a world where everyone is truly connected to themselves, happy, and living above heart-level? This is a possible reality. Let's make it real!

Remember, when it comes to gossip, just say "no comment."

Criticism

Hurt people hurt people. People that are hurting on the inside react and then hurt others with their words and actions.

Remember the mirror: if someone is talking meanly to you,

chances are they are just repeating the thoughts that are tearing them down inside their own minds. Don't listen to or believe those words. Recognize them for what they are: words the other person is feeling. It really has nothing to do with you. Imagine they are holding up a mirror and speaking those words to themselves. It's not about you. When you are living from your heart, you can see that all the words others speak are never about you. Remember the book *The Four Agreements*? One "agreement" is to never take anything personally. Other people's words and opinions are never really about you. It's all about them.

What if people's mean words were really a call to you for help? Maybe if we listen to what is going on inside them, we could be more kind and compassionate. What if when people are mean to us, we listened and responded to their plea for help?

When I find myself falling below heart-level, it's usually because of my own thoughts tearing me down. Things that personally bring me down internally are criticism, frustration (AKA unmet expectations), anger, overwhelm, procrastination, perfectionism, hiding and playing small, and breaking commitments. To daily combat all this, I remember who I am and what I stand for.

What do you stand for?

I stand for Peace. Love. Joy. Progress. Hope. Service. Truth. Celebration. Loving and serving others. Empowering women to be their best. I stand for you. I am here in your corner cheering you on. You so can do this, my friend. I love the woman you are becoming because I see your heart. I see your desire to show up and be the best version of yourself for you and your family. I see the deep love you have for yourself. I see your loving care for your children and the adoration in your eyes for your husband. I see that light in your eyes. You so can do this. You are worth it. You are amazing. You are here for a reason. You are here to lift and love others. You can do this! Let's do this together!

To help build ourselves up to withstand outside criticism, remember to focus on what you DO want.
- Be for something, and not against anything.
- Focus on what you DO want.
- Focus on creating, building, and improving.

Martin Luther King Jr., Rosa Parks, Mother Teresa, and Gandhi all had it right: Peaceful demonstrations are more powerful than force.

I will never be part of any "anti" group or campaign because that just focuses on the problem and blows it up bigger. What I will do is be part of a "pro" group. If you are pro-peace, I'm all for that. If you are pro-health, I am too! If you are pro-happiness, I'm on board!

Every human being matters a lot. We are all needed, loved, and divine. You matter. You are loved. You are divine. Say this out loud (even if just in a whisper): "I matter. I am loved. I am divine." You can choose to lift yourself and others UP with the words you use. The choice is yours. Your amazing life starts now. Make it happen!

World vision of peace in our homes

My vision, purpose, and mission: My vision is for validation, nurturing, and hope to naturally come from the people closest to those who need it most. Wouldn't it be amazing if everyone gave REAL support to the people they cared for so much?

Let's normalize the overcoming-depression conversation. I don't want people to have to come to me or another overcoming-depression specialist in order to get that validation, nurturing, and hope. What if we were all validation, compassion, and REAL support specialists for those closest to us whom we care for so deeply?

Eric and I have this within our marriage, and it is truly magical. It's so helpful! All I have to do is say to him, "I'm in Stage One," and he knows ONLY to give validation. He encourages me to validate my own feelings. It helps lift me every time. This also empowers him as the man to know how to help make it better. I know it's so frustrating for husbands to see their wives going through something difficult but having no clue how to help her make it better.

I imagine the husband of a wife experiencing depression trying to offer her help, but if she's down low, that specific help isn't helpful at that low stage. Frustrating? Yes. Feeling hopeless and just wanting to give up, he says to his wife, "Just get over it! Come on!"

On the flip side, now imagine the wife going to her husband saying, "I'm in Stage One. I don't want to feel better. I just don't care." The husband then knows, "OK, she's in Stage One. That means I help her validate." He asks her, "Honey, how are you feeling?" She responds, "Depressed. This is just too difficult." He lovingly asks, "May I offer support right now? May I offer a possible suggestion?" If she says yes, he responds, "Are you willing to play along with me for a second? Stand up, stomp your feet, and say, 'I feel depressed. This is too difficult, and that sucks!'"

After validation, they both know she now needs nurturing. She allows herself the space to nurture and care for herself. Her husband may offer support, like preparing dinner or taking the kids out to the park to give her more space. Or he may just encourage her to give herself permission to take time and space for herself.

Girls, our husbands really do love to help and support us. Sometimes they just don't know how. It's frustrating for them to try to help and then perceive their efforts as seemingly useless. On the flip side, it's so empowering when they know exactly HOW and WHEN to give that specific support. Share this book with your husband so you both can know how to best love and support each other through these truly difficult parts of life. You've got this! Do your best, and continue moving forward. You so can do this! Let's do this!

Tiny action

- Share something you've learned from this book with your husband or a friend.

Give yourself a high five and say, "I'm totally awesome!"

LETTERS OF LOVE

"Be a rock to others in need, be a rock of support to those who are facing critical issues, be a rock full of caring, … but also be a rock who recognizes that you also will experience times when you need to seek your own rock."
~ Byron Pulsifer

"I opened the letter, and I cried because someone out there really knew me and what I was experiencing. They showed me they truly care."

When you feel understood, you can then begin to build your foundation and move up toward healing again.

If you are experiencing depression or anxiety, dear sweet friend, I have written this letter just for you.

Letter of Love #1

To my dear friend experiencing depression and anxiety,

I see your comments. I see your pain. I see your hurt. I feel the depth of your sorrows and the pain in not knowing where to turn or what to do. My heart goes out to you. This sucks. I mean, this truly sucks! This pain is so deep; I would never wish it on my vilest enemy. I wish I could hug you, hold you, and tell you that all your feelings are so valid. It is OK to not feel OK. Totally valid. It is OK to not have it all together. It is OK to feel how you are feeling, because you are a valid human being and what you are feeling is so real to you. You really are feeling it, and ignoring those feelings won't make them go away. They actually get stronger the more you try to push them away, am I right?

This hurts. This hurts deeply. Nobody knows what is going on in your head, but those thoughts are tearing you down. Those feelings hurt so deeply that you may have just pushed them away to the point of feeling numb. You think, "I don't care." To any suggestions to get up and do something or change something, you just think, "I don't care." You couldn't will yourself to get up out of bed if you wanted to …

If I could, I would come clean your house, do some dishes, and just let you know you are cared about and cared for. You are heard, you are seen, you are a valid human being with real feelings, and those feelings are deeply hurting you right now.

Motherhood is too precious a time to be feeling so disconnected. You are heard, you are seen, you are totally valid. You are enough, and you are loved and cared for.

My dear, sweet friend, how may I best support you?

Letter of Love #2

To those precious women with thoughts of suicide/self-harm,

Life is really hurting you right now. You may have such depths of pain and sorrow, it is difficult to feel any of them, and you've just gone numb. You feel like, "I don't care." If you think of getting up and doing something, you think, "I don't care." It's not that you are heartless, it is that you feel so disconnected from yourself and everything else, that it feels like, "What's the point in trying?"

Letters of Love

You are not heartless; you just feel disconnected from your heart. You're hurting, and those feelings are valid. What you are feeling is real; those are real feelings. Whether it's truth on the outside or other people can't see it, those feelings are real to you. They may feel scary, feel deeply painful, and you feel like you never could be happy again. In fact, you see happy people and you despise them! It's so far from belief that you could ever be there that you resent anyone who is happy and loving their life. You might even strongly dislike me, and I'm OK with that. Why? Because if you can feel that against me, then you are feeling again! I am sincerely celebrating your progress!

I care enough about you to love you even when you might strongly dislike me. I care because I can see you; I see that you're hurting and you probably don't want to feel better (because you might be numb and don't want to feel anything!). I see you. I honor you. I validate that you feel sucky. Life sucks right now! Say it out loud, "I feel depressed, and that sucks!" "I feel depressed, and that feels crappy!"

Remember, the lies in your head are not your thoughts. These are thoughts expertly devised to pull you down into deeper disconnect. When they come into your head, simply say, "Thank you for sharing, but I choose to live."

There is no shame in how you are feeling. Allow yourself to feel, and take this one small moment at a time. If you can get through this, you can get through anything.

I love you, dear friend. I see and hear you. If I could help lessen this weight for you, I would. I sincerely ask you, how may I best support you?

Love,
A caring friend

If that was you (and I see you crying right now; I still cry when I read these letters), know that I truly meant every one of those words. If I can lighten your load just a little and help you see how truly amazing you really are, I would do anything to get these words to you when you need them most.

Tiny action

- Copy and paste parts or one of these letters and send to a woman who you know needs to hear these words! (Or write your own letter of love and validation and send it.)

Give yourself a hug and say, "I love myself, and I spread love to others."

YOU'VE GOT THIS, GIRL!

"Strength doesn't come from what you can do.
It comes from overcoming the things you once thought you couldn't."
~ Rikki Rogers

You now have the road map and more than enough tools to help support you and your loved ones on this journey called life. Better yet, you know exactly *when* to use these tips and tools to be the most supportive and effective. You now know how to lift and love, support and serve others around you who may be living below heart-level.

One last gift I will give you; here's a list of powerful affirmations arranged by stages for you to use any time you're feeling lower than you wish. Use these and focus daily on living above heart-level. You may just find yourself truly living and loving your life!

Affirmations for each stage

Stage 1:
- I feel depressed, and that feels crappy!
- I feel_____ and that feels_____.

Stage 2:
- I am more than enough.

- I am loved.
- I am deeply cared for.
- I am fully loved.
- I am nurtured.

Stage 3:
- If I can get through this, I can get through anything!
- If I can handle this, I can handle anything!
- I love my life! Exciting new things are just around the corner.
- Something exciting is as close as my next breath.
- I breathe in new hope, light, love, and excitement.
- My best days are yet ahead of me!

Stage 4:
- I am cared for.
- I care about others, and they care about me.
- Someone is waiting for me to ask for help.
- Someone is always willing to help me.
- Helping hands are reaching out to me.
- I am connected with other people at heart-level.

Stage 5:
- I love being in nature.
- I am connected to Mother Earth.
- I think I can. I know I can. I definitely can!
- I am enough.
- My efforts are totally worth it!
- I am making great progress!
- Let's do this!
- I've got this!

Stage 6:
- God loves me. I am His child.
- I strive to be my best.
- I am connected with the Divine.
- I am loved. I am worthy. I am worth it.
- I so can do this because I am amazing!!!
- I quickly forgive.
- I learn life's lessons quickly.
- I celebrate my life!

BOOM! Depression obliterated!

If you've moved through all these stages and fully reconnected at each level, you are probably feeling happy, joyful, and maybe even excited, peaceful, and amazing. Once reconnected, you are totally feeling like yourself again and living and loving from your heart. You are making progress and becoming better every day.

Thank you for reading this. Congratulations! You did it! If this helped you in any way, please share this book with a friend. It may just be the lifeline she's been searching for.

Your stories and triumphs are so amazing! I love celebrating your successes with you. Please send me your story of how this book helped you and what you've been able to do with this. I'd love to hear your stories of transformation and just plain feeling happy again. That's so amazing! Email me at RadiantLiving@live.com, or find me on Facebook (Heather Bailey) or on Instagram @EverBeBetter. Message me; I'd so love to hear from you and celebrate your journey with you!

We truly can live above heart-level (at least most of the time!). Living from your heart, loving your life, and being abundantly happy is truly possible. Let's use this to build ourselves UP and love and serve others. Together we can make our world amazing. Let's do this!

Love you!

The UNdepressed Heart

My Gift to You

I want to personally thank you for reading this book. I hope you have found it useful and will continue to use the tools found within its pages to change your life and the lives of your loved ones as you share the book with them.

Because you read this book, I want to offer you a "thank you" gift worth $100.00 in the form of a full treatment (similar to chiropractic but without cracking or popping; we get better results that way. And we do much more than align your spine. We do that, of course, and we release the stress your body is holding onto so you feel amazing! More info can be found at https://www.feelwelllivewell.com/b-e-s-t/). This treatment is available at any one of our clinic locations at NO charge for you and a guest. This does WONDERS for eliminating depression, so if you are ready to tackle depression once and for all, send an email to Office@FeelWellLiveWell.com with the subject "UNdepressed Heart" and let us know you've read this book. Include your name, the best phone number to reach you, and a note that you've read this book, and a staff member will be in touch shortly.

Life is too short to remain in the depths of depression. Email Office@FeelWellLiveWell.com right away and claim your FREE treatment.

Highly Recommended Happiness Reading

- *The 10 Habits of Happy Mothers*—Meg Meeker, MD
- *The Anatomy of Peace*—The Arbinger Institute
- *Being Unhappy Sucks, so STOP IT!*—Eric Bailey
- *Being Stuck Sucks, so STOP IT!*—Eric Bailey
- *Be Happy*—Hank Smith
- *The 7 Habits of Highly Effective Families*—Stephen R. Covey
- *7 Strategies for Wealth and Happiness*—Jim Rohn
- *Reset Your Child's Brain*—Victoria L. Dunckley, MD
- *Choosing Clarity*—Kimberly Giles
- *The Next Right Thing*—Emily P. Freeman
- *Daring Greatly*—Brené Brown
- *Living in Your True Identity*—Brooke Snow

If you liked this book, you'll also like "Being Unhappy Sucks, So STOP IT!"—a great book for men who struggle with depression.

Being *Unhappy* SUCKS

SO STOP IT!

Your Journey to Turning Stress, Anxiety, and Depression into Happiness Begins Here!

ERIC BAILEY

Acknowledgments

I thank my Savior for giving me this amazing life to live, love in my heart, and joy in my soul. I am grateful for the endless inspiration and guidance He gives me.

Thank you, powerfully positive messengers: I've learned decades of empowering wisdom both in person and from your written works. Thank you, Dr. Roland Phillips, Dr. M. T. Morter Jr., Kirk Duncan, Allie Casazza, Tony Robbins, Leslie Householder, T. Harv Eker, Dr. Willard Harley, John Bytheway, Oliver DeMille, Stephen R. Covey, Jim Rohn, Hank Smith, the Arbinger Institute, Mother Teresa, John C. Maxwell, Brad C. Wilcox, and many others!

About the Author

Heather Bailey lives with full purpose in her heart. She is vibrantly healthy and joyously alive. Many roles she lives in are as a mentor, massage therapist, healer, adoring wife to her husband, Eric, and loving mother of five beautiful children (with hope for more to come). She knows who she is at a deep level and holds a grand vision for where she is headed. Along with everyone else on this earth, she lives imperfectly and makes many mistakes, yet she is constantly growing, improving, and loving life more every day.

Made in the USA
Columbia, SC
31 January 2021